1001 WACKY THINGS TO DO!

1001 WACKY THINGS TO DO!

This book is full of zany ideas for cool kids!
Practical jokes, great gags and daft games!

ARCTURUS

ARCTURUS

This edition published in 2010 by Arcturus Publishing Limited
26/27 Bickels Yard, 151–153 Bermondsey Street,
London SE1 3HA

ISBN: 978-1-84837-520-8
CH001398EN

Author: Stephanie Clarkson
Illustrator: Darren McKee
Design and layout: Kate Wakeham
Editors: Mandy Archer and Kate Overy

Printed in Singapore

CONTENTS

Even the most dedicated wack-meisters need to stick to a few rules:

1 Practical jokes are only funny if the person you're pranking doesn't get hurt or upset - never take a trick too far.

2 When you're making any of the daft stuff in this book, get permission from an adult before cutting with scissors or using household substances for your wacky experiments.

3 Don't touch anything in the kitchen or even try to use an oven without asking the grown-ups (AKA the sensible people) that you live with first.

GAGS & PRANKS

This loopy list of **practical jokes** and **silly stunts** will send your family and friends running for cover. There's enough ammo in this chapter to keep pranksters sniggering for months!

One word of **warning** before you turn over - let these pages fall into the wrong hands and you could end up becoming the victim yourself!

1 Wanna drive your brother or sister totally **demented?!** Copy their every move from breakfast to bedtime, mimicking their speech, actions, even their clothes!

2 Use a pencil to push a small hole into an apple, then put it back in the fruit bowl. Drape a gummy sweet worm out of the hole – the longer the better. Now sit back, relax and wait for the screams to start!

TOP PRANK

3 Open an umbrella and turn it upside down. Fill it with a bunch of small, light objects such as the contents of a hole punch, then tidy it away. Whoever opens it next is in for some weird weather!

4 **Look as if you're about to say something really important - then simply walk away.**

5 On a cold day, wait until your annoying little brother or sister is busy doing their homework then shout:

IT'S SNOWING!

The deluded fools will be scrambling over to the window in seconds.

6 **Wander into a shop that sells reading glasses, then order a hamburger and fries whilst squinting as if you can't see properly.**

7 Trail a long piece of string along the pavement, round corners and up paths then watch a nosy parker try and follow it!

HA HA!!

8 In a crowded place sniff really hard then pull a face as if someone has let off a vile smell.

9 Set every alarm clock in your house to go off two minutes before the end of your mum's favourite TV soap.

10 Stand outside a public toilet looking lost, then ask passers-by where the nearest toilet is.

ANIMAL CAPERS

11

Gourmet goldfish

Going somewhere that has a fish tank? Get a carrot and cut a thin slice into a goldfish shape. Ask a grown-up to cook it for a few minutes until it's bendy. Hide the carrot-fish in the palm of your hand then wander over to the tank. Quickly dip your closed hand into the water and pull it out with the carrot-fish flapping between your fingers - pop the 'fish' into your mouth and munch!

GAGS & PRANKS

12 Next time you're having a sleepover nip upstairs and tie knots in all your mates' pyjama bottoms.

13 Tell your best friend that you can play the piano really well. When they roll up for a performance either flick on the demo mode on your keyboard, or just theatrically crash up and down the keys as if you're a concert pianist.

WARNING: WACKY WIND-UP!

14 Make out that you've lost your memory. Eye your folks suspiciously over the breakfast table and refuse to accept that you could possibly be related to them.

15 Pretend you can't speak a word of English all the way to and from school.

16 When you're next in the shopping mall, go up and ask random people for their autograph.

17 Drive your pals crazy by making out that you've got an amazing secret that you would like to tell them but can't.

ONE-MINUTE MADNESS

These gags are brief but bonkers!

18 Pretend that you've got an imaginary friend.

19 Hide every toilet roll in the house.

20 Fill a friend's shoes with crushed crisps!

21 Spend an entire day calling all your friends by each other's names.

22 Echo the last word of everyone's sentences.

23 Parents hogging the PC? Lure them out of the room by ringing the doorbell, then sneak in and place a small sticky note over the sensor of the mouse. When they get back they'll go nuts to discover that the mouse has suddenly 'broken'.

24 Next time someone puts some clothes in the tumble drier, replace the load with a bundle of dolls' outfits and see if they think that their washing has shrunk.

25 When your cat or dog next settles down for a nap, hide a walkie-talkie near it and retreat. As soon as one of the family comes in to give the pet a stroke shout **'geroff!'** into the walkie-talkie!

26 When your brother or sister jumps into the bath or shower, creep in and swipe their towel.

27 Dress up as a spy. Slip on your dad's overcoat and shades then walk down your street knowingly asking people 'do you have the secret package?'

GROSS OUT

28 Throw a truly gross fake sneeze. Put your fingers in water (green guacamole dip is even better!) then walk up quietly behind someone. Do a comedy sneeze whilst flicking the water or guacamole against their neck. Now run away – fast!

29 Secretly remove the batteries from the remote control for the TV, then sit and wait for the fireworks!

WEIRD OR WHAT?

30 Cup a boiled egg in your palm painted to look like an eye. Stagger around as if your eye has fallen out, covering one eye and moaning in pain.

31 Cover your face in your dad's shaving foam then smear a thick line of tomato ketchup across your cheek as if you've cut yourself in a terrible accident!

32 Put all the clocks in your house back by 37 minutes so that everyone's early all day.

33 Move into your brother or sister's room, lock stock and barrel! Swap all your toys over, change your bedding then make yourself comfortable in their space.

34 Slip a fake frog or other plastic pet into someone's sandwich. **Barf!**

GAGS & PRANKS

SCHOOL OF FUN

35 **Convince your friend that tomorrow is a compulsory non-uniform day.**

36 Pretend to be tearing up your mate's homework. Hold the short edge of a piece of paper between your pinched thumb and first finger of each hand. Pretend to tear it by holding it in front of your face and drawing the first finger of your right hand down the paper. At the same time make a **whooshing** noise with your mouth, keeping it hidden from view.

37 **Teacher's pest**
Fire homework missiles at your teachers as they head home after school.

Hey Sir ...
... homework delivery!

38 Write a note saying that you must be excused from Physical Education because you are allergic to the rubber soles of your training shoes.

39 Persuade your mates that a project that's not actually due for several weeks must be handed in first thing tomorrow!

40 ### Play the string trick
Find a kind-looking person and politely ask them to hold the end of a piece of string to assist with your school project on town planning. Disappear round a corner, unwinding the string while you go. Now ask another person if they would kindly hold the other end. You'll be in pieces by the time they get suspicious and start winding the string back towards each other!

41 Brighten up double maths by getting your mates to slowly pull their desks back a fraction every five minutes. By the end of the class your frazzled teacher will be agog as to how you all managed to slide yourselves back to the wall.

42 Get everyone to hum together behind your teacher's back, stopping the instant he or she turns to face you again.

TOP PRANK

43 When you get in casually tell your mum that you ate your lunch money at school. When she looks horrified and asks why, say 'well you said it was money for my lunch'.

44 Crack your mates up with this hilarious joke - the old ones are the best.

You: Knock knock
Friend: Who's there?
You: I Dunnop
Friend: I Dunnop Who?
You: HAHAHA YOU DONE A POO!!!!

45 **Try shuffling down the street with your best mate, pretending to hold a pane of glass between you. Watch people nervously move aside to let you pass.**

MIGHTY MESSY

46 Fill a bucket with shredded paper or tissue, then balance it on top of a door and wait for someone to come through.

47 Take a bite out of every apple in your fruit bowl then replace them with the chew marks artfully hidden.

48 **Freak out passers-by pretending to talk into a mobile phone - but you'll be holding nothing!**

49 Tape up the head hole on your brother's favourite jumper.

WOAHHHH...

50 Wipe charcoal around the eyepiece of your toy telescope, then persuade your little bro to go star-gazing.

51 Got a gullible mate? Pretend to be busy tinkering with something electronic then tell them to quickly go and ask an adult if they can have a long weight. They may take some time to get back to you (geddit?)!

GROSS OUT

52 Lift the toilet seat. Stretch plastic wrap over the bowl then lower the toilet seat again. Now wait for someone to take a pee! Tiptoe away before you totally wet yourself laughing!

53 Look worried and ask passers-by if they've seen your friends Teresa Green, Chris P. Bacon, Neil Down, Faye Kinnitt and Joe King!

HILARIOUS!

54 **Test your toilet humour!**
Write daft gags on sheets of toilet roll using permanent marker then float them in the bowl for the next visitor to enjoy. How about **'poo goes there?'** and **'the joke's on poo!'**.

55 Act like a talent show host blasting your friends' every move with withering put-downs such as **'you've just invented a new brand of torture'** or **'I presume there was no mirror in your dressing room.'**

17

GAGS & PRANKS

56 Next time your mate phones up for a chat, angrily tell him to get off the line. When he asks why, shout 'there's a train coming!' and abruptly hang up.

57 Milk monster!
When mum puts a new carton of milk in the fridge, sneak into the kitchen and pop a few drops of green food colouring into it. It'll look gruesome splattered on your dad's cereal!

58 Make a 'WET PAINT' sign then head out to the park. Prop it up on park benches, the bottom of swings and in front of doors – wherever it'll cause the most inconvenience!

Buzz...
Buzz...

59 Dress in yellow and black, buzz around, eat only honey and ask your parents the way to the hive.

60 Next time you're in a lift, salute and say 'WELCOME ABOARD' whenever anyone gets in.

18

61 Pretend you've had an arm transplant! Take your arms out of the sleeves of your jumper, cross them across your chest and poke them out of the wrong sleeves.

62 Start guffawing with laughter on public transport and see if anyone else starts laughing with you. If you can inspire at least three travelling titterers it's time to consider a career in showbiz!

PARENT ALERT!

63 Fill a large envelope with shaving cream. Slide the open end under a door where there is hard flooring instead of carpet on the other side. When you're sure that the person inside the room hasn't noticed, stamp on the fat part. Everything will be covered!

64 Here's a quick way to get more pocket money for the week. Bet your Dad he can't say a simple phrase three times over with no mistakes. Now get him to try this tongue twister:

'Are these watch straps Swiss wristwatch straps?'

Get ready to collect, he'll never manage it!

65 Cunningly pour cold tea into your friend's can of fizzy pop. Check out their face when they take their next sip!

66 Hide the left shoe of every pair in the house.

HEE HEE!

67 Take a loaf of white, unsliced bread and soak it overnight in a sink of water. By morning the bread will have absorbed every drop and have become swollen. Carry it carefully outside and throw it hard – you'll cover everyone and everything with gloopy white gunge!

68 Learn to do a comedy fall. Bring your right foot forwards as if to take a step, but instead, strike the back of your left foot with the toe of your right. As the toe connects with the other heel lunge forwards with your upper body and flail your arms as if you've been pushed.

WATCH OUT!

69 **Juggle on the bus with a set of invisible balls.**

70 Are your parents planning a posh dinner party? Then you can slip someone an eggy surprise! Ask an adult accomplice to fry you a few eggs. Hide the cooled eggs in a bag in your pocket, then slip one into each of the lucky guests' handbags.

ANIMAL CAPERS

71

Act like an owl – it's a hoot!

Kick off your shoes and take your arms out of the sleeves of your jumper. Crouch down so your feet are on the floor and your knees are bent up in front. Now pull the jumper over your legs and grasp the hem with your toes. Now push your fingers out under the hem like an owl's claws. Swivel your head and start acting like a **too-whit!**

20

OUTDOOR ANTICS

Do you dread those dreary days when your mum turfs you outside saying **'fresh air's good for you'**? Next time don't whine to come back in and watch telly - tuck this book under your arm and make your escape! These pages will get you **goofing around** in the garden, **cracking up** in the countryside and **playing pranks** in the playground.

OUTDOOR ANTICS

72 Measure your garden in mates – get a group of friends round, lie down head to foot and see how many of you it takes to reach from one end to the other.

TOP PRANK

73 Wanna sneakily soak your dad? Next time the garden sprinkler's set up, get a friend to stand on the hosepipe. Now complain to your dad that the sprinkler's stopped working. When he bends down to take a look, signal for your mate to jump off the pipe so that a rush of water soaks him!

74 **No snow?** Have a stinky sock-ball fight instead. Invite a friend over then chuck rolled-up pongy socks at each other.

75 **Find a park bench then turn your mate into a ventriloquist's dummy. Sit him on your knee, putting your hand up the back of his coat. Refuse to talk or answer questions without consulting him first.**

76 **Ouch-owzat!** Round up some mates and have a go at blindfold cricket! Find a soft ball 'cos you'll probably see more action than the bat.

77 Challenge your pals to an apple-rolling contest. Get on your knees, put hands behind your back then push the apple along the floor with your nose. Any cheaters should get piled on!

78 **We wish you a merry Marchmas**
Don't you wish it could be Christmas every day? Now it can! Create a festive treat for your neighbours by decorating a tree no matter what month it is. Choose a fir or spruce in your garden or park, dig out some tinsel and baubles and get carolling.

79 **Mum and dad confiscated your games console and forced you to join in the weekend family walk? Ruin everything by insisting on walking backwards. Next time they'll leave you in peace.**

80 **Make like Monet. Lay a long strip of paper along the pavement, get out your chalk then draw a portrait of yourself holding a strange object such as a pineapple or a wet fish. If anyone asks for an explanation, just shrug and tell them that it's your art.**

SILLY SCORE

81 **Make your own stilts!**
Loop some household string through the holes in the bottom of a couple of sturdy plastic plant pots. Make sure the string is long enough for you to grasp in each hand, put one foot on top of each pot then see how far you can travel on them without going flying. Pretty good? Race your friends to score points!

C'est magnifique!

23

ANiMAL CAPERS

82
What's up, Doc?
Why not be fluffy, furry, and infuriating for the day! Nibble on carrots like a pet rabbit, bark instead of talk, or make like a crazy cat and lap up your milk from a bowl!

83 Hot, bored and bothered? This wet 'n' wild game will cool you down in no time! Bowl balloons filled with water at a mate armed with a bat. (Note: best attempted with a cricket bat and not a flying mammal!)

84 Calling all bonkers dudes and dudettes! Have a day at the beach whatever the weather's like. Throw on your board shorts, flippers, diving gear and goggles then paddle in a puddle or take an early evening bath!!

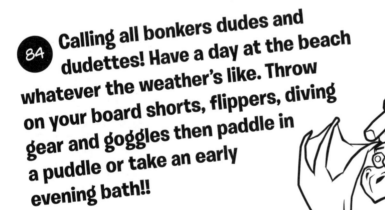

85 Rock out to a silent outdoor disco with your friends! Dress up in crazy gear, head to the park and bop away to imaginary tunes. Throw street dance moves to the blast of an invisible beat box, then finish up with a massive dance-off. Party on!

OUTDOOR ANTICS

86 Create a crime scene! Get one of your friends to play dead on the patio and draw a chalk line around them. Appoint yourself as chief detective then interview family members. Was your dad really in his office at 9.01 this morning or is he hiding something dark and disturbing...?

87 Camouflage your... leaves and grass. Wh... mum calls you in from the ga... sneak into the bushes and see h... long she takes to find you.

ONE-MINUTE MADNESS

You'll enjoy the great outdoors even more when you try these 60-second sillies...

89 Make a mud pie, then try compost cakes and soil sausage rolls.

90 See how many items of fruit you can hold without dropping them.

91 Have a 3-legged race... on rollerblades.

92 Roll down a hill from top to bottom.

93 Spin around on the spot 17 times with your eyes closed. Now try walking in a straight line.

88 Who said the best thing about being a fireman was sliding down the pole? Draw a raging inferno on the side of your house or garage with orange chalk. Fill loads of water bottles then start squirting to put the fire out!

OUTDOOR ANTICS

94 Sit on a park bench with a friend and pretend to be statues. Stay completely still until anyone approaches, then freak them out with a sudden jerky movement. *Gotcha!*

95 Have a weirdest walk contest with your mates. Put on your dad's boots, zone out like a zombie or slither like a snake. Whoever has the nuttiest moves wins.

96 Line-up all your friends in the street then perform a completely silent Mexican wave.

97 For the ultimate head rush have a handstand–off. How long can you outlast your buddy in the upside-down stakes before your eyeballs pop out?

SILLY SCORE

98 Give free-running a whirl! See if you can make it around your local playground or park without touching the floor - you may not be able to leap from tree to tree, but even raised kerbs count as being off the ground.

99 Next time your parents drag you and your little sis round town, pass the hours of boredom by playing 'Glimpse The Granny!' The rules are simple - just see how many little old ladies you can spot. Score **5 points** if she's wearing a hat, **10** for purple hair dye and **15** for a trolley on wheels. Go for gold and score **50 points** if you spot any wobbly false teeth!

100 Head to the park and try this game. One person is Hansel, one Gretel, the third plays the wicked witch. Hansel must sprint away from the group dropping a trail of pebbles behind him for Gretel to follow. One minute later Gretel should set off, with the witch being released one minute after that. Once the race is on, Gretel has got to catch up with Hansel before the baddie can nab them both.

101 Wait for a gusty day and go to the highest or most open piece of land you can find. Now lean into the wind with your arms outstretched in a superman pose.

DOUBLE  DARE

102 Ever tried extreme off-road wheelbarrow racing? It's the wilder version of wheelbarrowing where a friend holds your feet while you stagger forward on your hands. Find a hilly or swampy stretch of ground then go full pelt before you crash and burn in a muddy heap!

103 Stare and point at a building in the middle of town and see how many other people stop to have a gawp too. **DOH!**

104 Dog chewed your Frisbee in half? Make your own with a Styrofoam plate and paper cup. Put the cup in the centre of the plate and draw round the edge, then cut the circle out and wedge the cup into the middle of the plate. Decorate the foam with pens and you'll have a weighted Frisbee that's ready to fly!

OUTDOOR ANTICS

THESE BOOTS WERE MADE FOR WALKING...

105 Fill your mum's boots with soil and plant a beautiful flower arrangement in there. She'll be utterly irritated but unable to shout at you.

106 Round up your folks for a welly-flinging contest. Build a pile of walking boots, plastic shoes and waders, choose your weapon and get flinging!

107 Ever larked about with boots on your hands and gloves on your toes? C'mon have a go - you know you want to!

108 Scoop jelly into your dad's boots, then retreat to a safe distance when he decides to get up and pull them on. The poor guy will be so freaked he'll probably throw a wobbly!

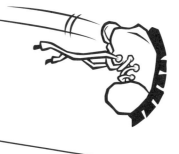

109 Start a new trend for summer! Cut the toes out of a boring pair of old rubber boots and wear them as sandals. Tell your mates that you've invented bandals. Then try turning them into blip blops...

GROSS OUT

110 Mix up your favourite fruit squash then have a drinking race using your wellies as bizarre goblets. When you've gulped down your drink stick the empty welly on your head to prove it!

SILLY SCORE

111 Pull on some rubber boots then find the biggest, sludgiest, muddiest puddle you can. Jump in it then shout for someone to call for help as you're stuck in a swamp. See how quickly someone comes to your rescue – the shorter the time the higher the score.

112 **Put another snowy shrimp on the barbie, mate!**
Snow is perfect welly-wearing weather! But confuse the neighbours by persuading your parents to fire up the barbeque mid-winter, then munch burgers and hot-dogs in your shorts, t-shirt and boots.

OUTDOOR ANTICS

113 Dress up as Batman and run round the streets shouting

TO THE BATMOBILE!

WHICH WAY TO GOTHAM CITY?

in a determined voice.

114 Secretly attach a tiny blob of mud to the bottom of a blade of grass. Hold the grass by the tip and bet your buddy he cannot catch the grass between his thumb and forefinger when you drop it without warning. You'll get him every time!

WARNING: WACKY WIND-UP!

115 Mum dragging you round the supermarket again? Jump after the trolley like a kangaroo shouting 'boiiing, boiiing!' in an Aussie accent. She'll be bribing you with treats quicker than you can say 'bonzer bouncing, mate!'

116 Silly Sumo!
Have a sumo match, stuffing sofa cushions inside your clothes to add extra bulk.

117 It's a dog's life
Give your dog the other end of the lead for a change. Now loop the collar end round your ankle and let him take you for a stroll.

118 Wimble-don't
Set up an imaginary lawn tournament, complete with invisible bats, balls and net! Throw outrageous trick shots, argue with the umpire, then throw a whopping tantrum at the final score.

119 **Rock out man!** Find a crowded shopping mall, drop your hat on the floor like a busker and play the air guitar like a rock star.

120 Offer to treat your parents' car to a wash – then wander outside armed with your mum's hairdryer and a bottle of her most expensive shampoo.

121 **Next time you're in the park, run round hugging trees. If anyone questions you, look baffled and keep going.**

122 Try your hand at Mexican wrestling. Make yourself a mask or tie a scarf around your forehead. Now put your underwear over the top of your trousers and give yourself a crazy name. Use your imagination to think up an alias to suit your fighting style. The aim is to get your opponent to the floor and hold him down for 10 seconds.

123 **Set up a fishing pole on the edge a frozen pond to confuse passers-by – just don't walk on the ice!**

124 Challenge your pals to a reverse race, where the aim of the game is to finish last!

125 Fill your underwear or your socks with conkers and see if anyone's on the ball enough to notice that you've changed shape.

126 Make a sign and wave it at people, animals and any loud weather that

SILENCE IN THE PARK

comes your way when out for a stroll. People will think you're mad!

127 When you're out on your bike, wave at everyone you pass. Check out the people that wave back then look confused as they try to work out how the heck they know you.

128 Give a grass concert. Pick a long blade of grass and pinch it lengthways between your thumb knuckles. Form an O with your mouth and press the knuckles against your lips. Blow hard. See how many tunes you can belt out.

ANIMAL CAPERS

129 Try catching a butterfly with your bare hands – you'll never do it, but you'll have fun trying!

130 Why walk when you can drive? Pretend you're at the wheel of an awesome Porsche when you're next out with your mates – change gears, flick the indicators and wind down the window to talk to people.

32

131 Form an aerobatic team... on the ground. Start running in a V formation with your pals, then peel off at intervals. Attempt a dangerous mid-air flyby or a roly-poly loop-the-loop!

132 Pretend you're a celebrity for the day. Wear sunglasses and a large hat then prod people on the chest demanding 'don't you know who I am?'!

GROSS OUT

133 Always wanted to star in a reality TV show? Set up your own gruesome endurance challenge for your mates. Ask blindfolded contestants to stick their hands in buckets containing mud, worms and pond weed, or soak their feet in cold baked beans.

134 **Roll up, roll up, roll up,** the Batty Olympics are taking place in a backyard near you! Get each of your pals to pull on comedy sports gear and you're ready to go. Try hurdling over piles of hoodies, tossing wet sponges or doing relays armed with a piece of cooked spaghetti. Line up for a medal presentation at the end, dishing out wooden spoons, rubber gloves, egg whisks and other essential household objects to the lucky winners!

33

135 Pretend that your dad's prize rosebushes are scary plants that eat human flesh. The garden's not looking so boring now is it?! Chop off a few heads if you dare... it's self-defence after all!

136 **Play Spitman!**
Borrow your parents' video camera then film each other projectile-spitting a stream of water. You do this by hiding a garden hose behind your body and filming from the side so it looks as if the water is spewing directly out of your mouth. They'll either be really impressed or totally freaked out!

ONE-MINUTE MADNESS

These five cool quickies are too mad to miss!

137 Moonwalk like an astronaut across the front garden.

138 Sprint down your street in slow-motion.

139 Drink some fizz then have a burping contest.

140 Play tennis with a hard-boiled egg instead of a ball.

141 Tie your shoelaces together then see how far you can walk.

142 Blow a rainbow! On a day with bright, low light, turn your back so the sunlight streams over your shoulder. Fill your mouth with water so your cheeks bulge like a greedy hamster. Now squash your cheeks suddenly while shaking your head from side to side so a fine mist sprays out in front of you - you'll see your own personal rainbow.

DOUBLE TROUBLE

Mischief with a mate is twice the fun - **guaranteed!** In this chapter you'll find the inspiration you need to create the perfect **daft double act**. All the classic gags are here, plus some brand-new **time wasters** that'll leave you both in stitches!

DOUBLE TROUBLE

143 Become your best buddy for the day! Swap clothes, hairstyles and names with your best friend, see if you can mimic their tone, accent and funny mannerisms.

144 Pretend you're in the Tour de France – pedal like mad around the house, squirt yourselves with water when hot, overtake each other on bends and award the winner a yellow t-shirt. **Vive Le Champion!!**

146 **Build your own crazy golf course, using toys for tunnels and paper cups for holes.**

147 **Don't chat, just rap** Pick a style of music and sing everything to each other in that style all day. Have a go at rhyming like a hip hop star or bash your friend's eardrums with loud outbursts of opera.

SILLY SCORE

145 Commentate on everything your friend does as if he or she's competing in a mega-serious sporting event: **'she's coming into the bedroom and is sitting down on the bed… no, she doesn't seem to be sitting for long. She's off! Now she's done a perfect loop straight into the bathroom. GGGOOOOAAALLL!!!!'.** Give yourself **1** point when you mate gets mildly annoyed, **5** when they go red in the face and **10** when they are driven totally insane!

148 Count each other's freckles and moles. Who has the most? Play dot-to-dot with your beauty spots, drawing crazy pictures on each other's bodies. Just remember to use pens that wash off afterwards!

149 Ribbit, ribbit! Leap frog over each other in turn all the way into town or up to the park and back again.

150 Pretend to be your parents. You'll need to tell your siblings off - a lot!

151 Pull out your mobile or camcorder then make your own pop video. Mime outrageously to your favourite tune in odd locations, then edit the clips together in a You Tube style!

152 Design you own brand new comic starring your new heroes – what crazy adventures will they have together?

Slugman to the rescue!

153 Is it a bird? Is it a plane?
No, it's Slugman! Make up your own crazy super-hero name then devise some demented powers for yourself. Slugman can suck his enemies to death, what can your alter ego do?! Now rope in a mate to be your sidekick... make special costumes to suit your hero and helper and race around together saving the world from baddies.

ONE-MINUTE MADNESS

It's amazing what silliness two can have in 60 seconds!

154 Have a breath-holding contest. Who can last longest without bursting?

155 Feelin' serious? Hold a frown for as many seconds as you can before your mate makes you laugh.

156 Have a bunk-bed battle. Launch teddy missiles and sock bombs at your opponent in the other bunk until they surrender to your demands.

157 Time each other to see how long you can stare without blinking - not as easy as it seems!

158 Swap right shoes with each other then go for a walk.

159 Take turns being each other's servant or butler for the day. See how demanding you can be as the master, and how efficient and crawling you can make the snivelling servant.

MIGHTY MESSY

160 Do a fake tandem sky dive! Strap your friend onto your front, put a backpack on your back, assume a skydiving position then enjoy the ride.

161 Set up a stall outside your house selling mud pies. Dirt doughnut or sludge sponge for anyone???

162 WHO'S THE PARROT?
Drive everyone crazy - twice! Take it in turns for one of you to echo what the other one says as they say it... say it. Might take a little while to get it right, but it's well worth the effort... well worth the effort!

163 Speak to each other all day in a French, Italian or Russian accent. Allo! Allo!

DOUBLE TROUBLE

164 Time for a simultaneous hairdressing contest! Sit in front of each other cross-legged then see who can do the craziest style within 10 minutes. Use gel, clips and hairbands... but give the scissors a miss!

165 Take each other's favourite toy and see how many times you can be photographed with it in exotic or unexpected places.

166 Borrow your dad's can of shaving foam then see who can create the longest and fuzziest Father Christmas beard.

Ho, ho, ho!

DOUBLE TROUBLE

167 Make up a secret language. Try sending the first letter of each word to the back and adding in an 'ay'. 'Hello' becomes 'ellohay', 'watcha' becomes 'atchaway' and 'don't speak English' translates into 'on'tday peaksay, nglisheay'.

168 Weave a spider's web. Stand at opposite sides of the room and throw a ball of string forward and back to each other. Anchor the thread round some furniture or a toy, then change position and do the same.

Double  Dare

169 Paint each other's faces with strange and wild make-up - daub on layers of lipstick, outrageous streaks of blusher and the sparkliest shades of eyeshadow you can lay your hands on. When you're done, decide which one of you is brave enough to go out for a walk!

170 Start a really weird fan club for an obscure interest like gargling or foot sniffing.

171 Make up your own cheerleading team then think up a crazy routine. When you're next at the park, stun the local five-a-side team by offering your 'support'! Be brave, boys – this one's for you, too!

SILLY SCORE

172 Mark each other out of 10 for everything you do in a day! Try to make each movement as over-the-top as possible, from the way you get out of a chair to your style of walking through the door. Extra marks should be awarded for artistic impression, effort and acrobatic ability. Write big numbers on pieces of A4 paper, then ask your folks to hold them up as you glide past.

173 Form a comedy double act. You'll need a straight man and a zany side-kick. Which is which? Draw on comedy moustaches and think up some gigglesome gags.

174 Recreate your class with old toys - make Barbie the nice art teacher and that horrible-looking old dog with half its fur missing your bumbling principle or headmaster! Instead of grumpy dinner ladies, line up a canteen full of toy soldiers, then act out all the naughty pranks you wish you could do at school!

DOUBLE TROUBLE

CIRCUS SKILLS

175 TAKE A WALK ON THE WILD SIDE AND RECREATE THE BEST ANIMAL ACTS FROM TIMES GONE BY. PRETEND TO BE A LION AND HIS LION-TAMER, TWO LUMBERING ELEPHANTS OR A PERFORMING SEAL AND HIS TRAINER.

176 Make your own fantasy flea circus! Create and paint an arena inside an empty cardboard box, then make some tiny paper carts and balls to roll. Dress yourselves up as ringmasters and invite an audience to watch the micro-animals in action.

177 Lay a skipping rope across the lawn, then hold up an open umbrella. Pretend to do a precarious tightrope walk while your friend runs nervously beside you, getting ready to catch you if you 'fall'.

178 TAKE TURNS TO BE A HORSE AND RIDER. SEE HOW LONG YOU CAN LAST BEFORE EACH HORSE COLLAPSES UNDER THE WEIGHT!

179 Pretend to be the strong man. Use a broom or long stick with two balloons or beach balls tied at either end. Paint on a twirly moustache. Strain to lift the heavy weights, grunting and groaning a lot, while the ringmaster shouts out encouragement.

180 ## Raise your own big top!

Persuade your dad to set the family tent up in the back garden, pull back the flysheets and invite your mates to sit around the 'ring'. Sawdust salvaged from the rabbit hutch and scattered over the floor will set the scene perfectly for your two-man show.

181 ### Tumble time!
Practise doing circus couple cartwheels on a soft patch of grass. One of you goes into a handstand holding onto the other person's ankles with your hands instead of putting them on the floor. The upright person then holds onto your ankles with their hands. Get cartwheeling, humming circus tunes as you turn!

182 Fancy clowning around? A circus isn't a circus without a pair of slapstick jokers in over-sized shoes! Hold your granddad's trousers up with braces, pull on some inappropriate footwear, then use your mum's make-up to give each other red noses. Now all that's needed is to work out a routine.

DOUBLE DARE

183 Grab some playing cards, then challenge your bud to a game of forfeit snap. The person who says 'snap' quickest not only wins the other's cards, they also get to dare the other person to do something crazy. Kissing the cat, armwrestling your mate's sister and eating without using hands all make killer forfeits!

184 Play shadow jumping! Go out for a walk on a sunny day and see if one of you can jump on the other's shadow head, while the first person runs around like a loony trying to escape you.

185 Throw your friend a 'surprise' Happy Tuesday party. Random stuff rocks!

186 Have a cracker-eating contest! See who can eat the most without needing a glug of water.

187 Make up a country and declare yourselves King and Queen. Decide on the laws of the land and punish anyone who dares to thwart them.

188 Turn the sound down on the TV and do idiotic voice-overs for the latest natural history programme...

189 Having a sleepover? Try staying awake all night. Do it together or work shifts to see in the dawn.

190 Practice catwalk modelling down the landing wearing your sister's clothes!

PARENT ALERT!

191 Barricade yourselves into your bedroom using as much stuff as possible. See how long you can stay put before your mum sends your dad out to fetch a battering ram!

192 Use fabric paint to decorate old t-shirts with arrows pointing to each other and the slogan:

I'm with stupid! ⟶

Now sidle up to people in town and see how long you can stand next to them before they catch on!

193 Be your friend's arms for the day. Get them to stand with their hands behind their back, then push your arms through the gaps. Make sure you scratch their heads, wave to people and gesticulate madly as they talk!

194 Have a pyjama party – in the middle of the day. Get your pjs on, have a midday midnight feast in bed, and tell spooky ghost stories.

DOUBLE TROUBLE

195 Go prehistoric. Become your favourite dinosaurs then go on a raucous rampage all round the garden or playground.

196 Play your favourite board game blindfolded. Don't worry about winning, keeping track of the dice is going to be hard enough!

ONE-MINUTE MADNESS

Is your mate as mad as you? Find out with one of these short 'n' snappy challenges!

197 Buy a doughnut each. See who can eat theirs without having to lick their lips.

198 Everywhere that you normally run, try skipping instead.

199 Feed each other a banana with your eyes closed. Very messy!

200 Have a face-pulling contest.

201 Go into town then randomly shout people's names until someone turns round.

202 Make up a new word that no-one has ever spoken before, then use it in conversation between yourselves when talking in front of others.

203 Become self-trained mountaineers! Try moving around the downstairs of your house without touching the floor at any time.

GROSS OUT

204 Make each other a revolting drink by mixing tea, juice and fizzy pop. Who's got the stomach to finish their whole glass? Extra respect is due for a big burp at the end!

205 Create your own 'flog' - a friendship blog on the Internet. Ask an adult to set it up, then get flogging. Document all your wildest adventures to entertain and amuse your mates.

206 **Sock it to 'em!** Take your shoes off and try to remove your opponent's socks without losing your own. One small catch - you are not allowed off your hands and knees. You are also banned from trying to hold onto your own socks during the rumble!

207 **Sshh!** Don't say a word. Only communicate with each other by letters and notes.

208 **Have a foot-wrestling contest**
Lie down on your backs with your bare feet towards each other, then bend your knees, raise your legs and place the soles of your feet against your friend's soles. Hands stay flat on the floor by your side. On the count of 10 push as hard as you can. Who's gonna give way first?

209 If you are girls pretend to be boys and the other way round. 'Boys' should swagger, talk in deeper voices and play with action figures. 'Girls' should hold tea parties, try on pretty dresses and sit down and giggle a lot.

210 Dare each other to touch the bugs that freak you out the most - try worms, beetles and earwigs. Go on... face your fears!

211 Pretend your right elbow is superglued to your friend's left elbow. See how much you can do during the day superglued together - best break off for the toilet, though!

212 Atten - shun!
Mount a thumb war. Hold each other's right hands, grippin fingers but leaving your thumbs free. Shout **'one, two, three, four, I declare a thumb war'** then try to pin down your friend's thumb using your own. Fingers must stay gripped and hands held vertical at all times. The winner is the person who can pin the other's thumb down for 10 excruciating seconds!

213 Send each other mindless silent messages using flags in different positions! First make up your own secret code of insulting signals such as 'you look like a baboon's bottom'! Now grab two flags each, stand at each end of the garden and practise signing them out.

silly secret

MAD SCIENCE

There's a **crazy scientist** bubbling away inside all of us! Now's the time to channel your inner Frankenstein and release yours. Grab a white coat, start **cackling** like a maniac and you're ready to go! This chapter is **fizzing** with gravity-bending stunts, brain-scrabbling experiments and amateur **explosions**.

MAD SCIENCE

214 Make self-inflating balloons! Add three teaspoons of baking soda to a balloon using a piece of paper rolled into a funnel. Now fill a clean empty bottle one third full with vinegar. Fit the balloon over the bottle opening and hold it up so the baking soda falls into the vinegar. The carbon dioxide will inflate the balloon before your very eyes!

Fizzruptions!

216 It's amazing what fun you can have with a large bottle of Diet Coke, half a pack of Mentos and a funnel. Stand the Diet Coke upright and use the tube to drop all the Mentos in at the same time. Now run like mad before the gigantic geyser splatters you!

217 Ever seen gravity-free water? Put a piece of cardboard over a glass of water, making sure no air bubbles can get in. Turn the glass upside down and remove the hand holding the cardboard. The cardboard and water should stay put. With no air inside, the pressure from outside the glass is greater than the pressure of the water inside.

GROSS OUT

215 Fill half a cup with boiling water, then add three teaspoons of gelatin. Now drop in four tablespoons of glucose syrup. Stir the mixture again. As the mixture cools add small amounts of water, a few drops at a time. Check out the sticky protein strands – they look exactly like real snot.

Aaaaachooo!

218 Fill two clear tumblers with the same amount of water, one cold and one hot. Ask your friend to choose one of the glasses, then to guess which will change colour quicker. Put one drop of food colouring into both tumblers. The food colouring should spread faster through the hot water every time.

ONE-MINUTE MADNESS

Crazy chemistry and bonkers biology is so much more fun in your own home...

219 Plug in a hairdryer, put it on the highest setting and point it into the air. Place a ping pong ball above the dryer then watch it float and bounce.

220 Make instant quicksand! Mix a cup of cornflour with half a cup of water in a large plastic tub. Stir it just before you use it. Now have fun making small toys sink!

221 Try and fold your tongue into a U-shape. A gene controls whether or not you'll be able to do it.

222 Fill a clear glass to the brim with warm water. Take an ice cube and lower it in. Watch the water level as the ice cube melts and you'll find amazingly that the glass doesn't overflow.

223 Backcomb your hair until it stands on end and open all the buttons on your shirt. Stagger into the front room while your folks are watching TV, telling them that there's been a terrible explosion in your bedroom. Your dad will be up those stairs in two seconds flat!

224 Place an empty tin can on its side then rub a balloon up and down your jumper. Hold the balloon close to the can and watch as it rolls towards it – move the balloon away and the can will follow, too!

MAD SCIENCE

MAD SCIENCE

225 Recite this nursery rhyme in science class...
Mary had a little lamb, its fleece was white as snow because all the coloured light was reflected in one go.

226 Cut an ice cube in half without touching it! Take a piece of fishing line and tie a weight to each end. Turn a plastic container upside down then place the ice on top. Rest the fishing line over the ice cube so that the weights are left dangling over the sides. The weights will pull the string through as the pressure melts the ice!

227 Get your hands really soapy, place your palms together and then pull your hands apart making sure your thumbs and index fingers stay in contact throughout. You'll see a kaleidoscope of swirling colours!

PARENT ALERT!

228 Create your own mad lab! Commandeer a corner of your dad's shed and kit it out with your mum's Tupperware collection. Make homemade test tubes out of old vitamin tablet tubes. When your parents storm in to get their stuff back, tell them that it's very important science homework!

229 Tickle your taste buds
Find a small piece of peeled potato and a small piece of peeled apple that are the same size and shape. Bet your friend that they can't tell the difference with their eyes closed and nose pinched. It's harder than it sounds!

230 Blow up a balloon and hold it close to your ear, then tap very lightly on the other side. The balloon will magnify the sound so that your ear hears it much more loudly than it really is!

232 Take a heavy football and balance a tennis ball on top, holding one hand under the big ball and the other on top of the small one. Suddenly let go with both hands at the same time. The tennis ball will bounce off the football and fly into the air!

231 Try this... fill a bowl with water then place a small cup in the bowl so it's half-submerged. Now turn the cup upside down then try and lift it straight up out of the water. No matter how tough you are, it won't wanna come!

MAD SCIENCE

233 Attack your little brother with a mini-para! Cut a large hexagonal shape out of a plastic bag. Now snip a small hole near the edge of each of the six sides. Attach six pieces of string of the same length to each of the holes and tie the other ends ...

OPERATION HEADPLUNGE

... of each piece of the string to a small action figure. Tiptoe to the top of the stairs and wait til your bro walks through the hallway then let fly!

53

MAD SCIENCE

234 Move water between glasses without touching them! Take an empty glass and a glass filled with water. Twist some paper towels together to form a rope. Put one end of the towels into the water-filled glass and let the other dangle over the empty glass. Before long the empty glass will start to fill with water!

235 Make your own fizzy pop!
Squeeze the juice of some lemons into a tumbler and add an equal amount of water. Stir in a teaspoon of baking soda and add some sugar to make your own bubblicious lemonade!

236 Make yourself a realistic looking volcano out of card. Place it on a tray and sprinkle some baking soda underneath it. Now pour in some vinegar and enjoy the bubbly eruptions!

237 Try the bent straw trick!
Fill a glass half full with water and add a drinking straw. Now stun your little sis by getting her to look at the glass from the side, focusing on the point where the straw enters the water. She'll gasp out loud, claiming that the straw looks completely bent!

MIGHTY MESSY

238 Get your mum or dad to help you make some silly putty! Pour some craft glue into a pastic cup. Add one tablespoon of water and stir. Now add a tablespoon of liquid starch then one drop of food colouring. Gather the gloop into a ball and give it a good squeeze. Leave it to dry on a piece of wax paper then enjoy your funny putty!

DOUBLE DARE

239 Challenge your mate to fold a piece of paper in half more than nine times. They'll never be able to do it - it's virtually impossible!

MAD SCIENCE

240 Find out why we don't wear black in summer. Wrap a piece of white paper around a drinking glass using an elastic band. Do the same with a piece of black paper on an identical glass. Leave the pair in the sun for a couple of hours. The black glass's water will be much hotter.

241 Add enough milk to cover the bottom of a baking tray. Drop some food colouring into the centre. Now add a couple of drops of washing-up liquid and watch the colours explode!

242 Make easy peasy invisible ink! Squeeze lemon juice into a bowl and mix in a few drops of water. Now write a message on a sheet of white paper using a cotton bud dipped in the mixture. Wait for the juice to dry and when you are ready to reveal your secret message heat the paper by holding it close to a light bulb.

YOU MUST BE JOKING!

243 Make your mates titter in science class with this daft gag.
Teacher: What is the formula for water?
Student: H, I, J, K, L, M, N, O
Teacher: That's not what I taught you.
Student: But you said the formula for water was H to O!

eggstraordinary eggsperiments

244 **Make a rubber egg! Put a hard-boiled egg with the shell still on into a cup of white vinegar. Let it sit for two days then remove it and gently rinse the shell off. Now try bouncing it! The egg's shell has been 'eaten' by the vinegar, leaving the rubbery membrane behind.**

245

Ask a friend if they can tell the difference between two eggs without smashing them. Take one hard-boiled one and one raw out of the fridge and spin them.

Sshhh!

The hard-boiled egg will always spin while the raw one wobbles as the white and yolk slop around inside the shell.

silly secret

246 **Bet your dad he can't balance an egg on either of its ends. He's doomed to fail!** When it's your turn, hold the egg pointed end upwards and hit the wider end gently on the table so that the shell cracks but doesn't split. Time to collect your winnings...

247 Suspend an egg in water. Take a tall, clear glass and half fill it with water. Stir in six tablespoons of salt. Carefully top the glass almost to the brim with more water and gently lower the egg in. It will float gracefully in the centre.

248 **Egg in a bottle**
Take a large hard-boiled egg with the shell removed and a glass bottle with an opening slightly smaller than the egg. Place a small piece of paper in the bottle together with a lit match. Quickly put the egg on top of the bottle so that the opening is closed. You'll be stunned to see the egg magically squeeze itself into the bottle!

MAD SCIENCE

249 Put your hand on a table with your middle finger tucked back underneath your palm. Now try lifting all of your fingers without allowing your middle digit to budge an inch. **It's impossible!**

250 Mastermind your own rocket launch. Attach a couple of lengths of ribbon to a cork with a pin. Add half a cup of water and the same amount of vinegar to a small empty bottle of pop. Place a teaspoon of baking soda in the centre of a square of kitchen towel and twist the ends to keep the soda from falling out. Head outside with your launch crew and drop the paper towel into the bottle then wedge the cork on tight. Stand back and watch…

SILLY SCORE

251 Make some racing raisins! Fill a glass with ginger ale, then you and a friend each drop in three raisins. The fruit will sink to the bottom then begin to rise up to the top. The first one to the top gets 3 points, second 2 points and third 1 point.

WHOOSH…

BANG!

58

252 **My glass is super full**
Fill a glass to the brim with water. Bend down so that you are at eye level with the rim of the glass, then carefully add more a few more drops. You should be able keep going until the water level is higher than the top of the glass! This is due to the millions of tiny water molecules holding on to each other.

253 Float a soap boat. Cut a small piece of cardboard into the rough shape of a boat. Drop it into a bowl of water and it won't go anywhere. Now turn the boat over and put a drop of soap under the back end. It'll zip across the bowl in no time.

MAD SCIENCE

WARNING: WACKY WIND-UP!

254 Wanna tell your brother he's a jerk? Put a couple of drops of liquid hand soap into a cup. Use your finger to write a message on the mirror in the bathroom. Make sure it is thin enough to be invisible. Next time your bro takes a dip the writing will magically appear in the steamy mirror.

255 Make your arm magically float into the air by standing next to a wall with one hand pressed against it. Push your arm as hard as you can against the wall for a count of 30. Now step away from the wall and relax both arms. Your arm will start to rise whether you want it to or not!

59

MAD SCIENCE

256 Fill a bowl with water. Put a napkin inside a glass – make sure the napkin is crumpled and really squashed into the glass. Place the glass upside down in the bowl of water making sure it goes all the way down. Now take the glass out and place it right side up. Feel the napkin – it's dry!

WEIRD OR WHAT?

257 Is water heavier or lighter than oil? To find out fill a glass until it's three-quarters full with vegetable oil. Now drop in an ice cube. The ice is less dense than oil so it will float on top, but as it melts the water will sink below.

258 This knotted bones trick will fox your friends. Take some thin chicken bones and drop them in vinegar for a day. When you take them out again they'll be soft. Tie them in a knot and leave them on a worktop until they get hard again. When they see this evidence your pals will think you're a hulk!

259 **Gravity giggle** Put Newton's Law to the test. When your dad is next seen relaxing in the garden, tiptoe out and drop an apple on his head. When he goes bananas, say it was an experiment for your science homework!

260 Has your mum been given some boring white carnations? Give her the shock of her life by placing them in a vase half-filled with water and 20 drops of your favourite food colouring. The petals will magically change shade!

261 Wanna know how a plane stays up? Hold a strip of paper by one end slightly below your mouth, then blow hard over the top of the paper to lift up the other end. Air over the wings of a real plane creates a vacuum that sucks the vehicle upwards in the same way.

MAD SCIENCE

262 Turn on the tap so that water runs out in a small, steady stream. Charge a comb by running it through long, dry hair several times or rub it hard on a woolly jumper. Slowly bring the comb close to the running water and the stream will begin to magically 'bend'.

263 Rub a balloon on your hair then take a look in the mirror. **Freaky!**

264 This travelling flame trick is a corker, but you'll need an adult helper. Light a candle and have another lit candle ready nearby. Blow out the first candle then quickly place the other flame into the smoke. The second flame should travel down the smoke and re-light the first candle.

DOUBLE DARE

265 Challenge a buddy to tie a knot in a piece of string without letting go - they'll never be able to. The trick is to fold your arms first before grabbing the ends of the string. Carefully unfold your arms and you've tied the knot without letting go!

266 Can you pick up an ice cube without touching it? Drop an ice cube into a cup of water then lay a piece of string across the cube. Now sprinkle table salt onto the string. Within a few seconds you'll be able to lift the string with the ice cube attached!

267 Stack some coins on a table then put your finger on another coin. Push your coin towards the stack and let go of it so that it slides and hits the stack with force. It will knock the bottom coin out without causing the stack to topple!

268 Scribble crazy formulae into a notebook, Einstein-style. If any of your folks try and ask you about it, flounce out as if you're surrounded by utter cretins.

WEIRD OR WHAT?

269 Punch three small holes near the bottom of an empty juice carton. Fill it with water and you'll see three separate streams exit from the holes. Now pinch the streams together. Hey presto! You've tied a water knot.

BEHIND CLOSED DOORS

Rainy day? Mates out of town? No problem. This chapter will show you dozens of ways to wackily while away the hours on your own! Every suggestion is **100% goofy** - guaranteed to get you giggling when everybody else you know is being sensible. Didn't think you could get any more **immature?** Just wait and see!

270 Create a security system for your bedroom. String a length of fine cotton at ankle level across your doorway. If it gets broken you'll know at once that your pest of a brother's been trespassing in your room.

271 See how long you can go without saying the words 'cool', 'OK' or 'like'.

GROSS OUT

272 Make a sticky tape scar! Stick a length of tape across your cheek and sponge it with water until the cellophane backing detaches, leaving just the adhesive behind. Pinch the skin together and it will suddenly look like a wound. Now daub on some ketchup 'blood' splodges.

273 Give yourself a high five every time you do anything well. Remember you're the judge – even eating an obscene amount of cereal at breakfast could deserve a pat on the back.

274 Go camping in your bedroom
Make a tent with your duvet, hum camping songs, snaffle an indoor picnic and protect your camp from bears (of the cuddly variety).

ANiMAL CAPERS

275

Create a wildlife chorus...

Practice hooting like an owl by clasping your fingers together and blowing through the hole between your thumbs. Make weird and eerie whale noises or laugh like a hyena.

276 Throw yourself a birthday party. Make a cake, draw a card, sing happy birthday to yourself several times over and sulk if your mum and dad haven't got you a present.

BEHIND CLOSED DOORS

278 Create your own crazy dictionary crammed with made-up words. Give common objects the most nutty-sounding names you can think of. Why ask for a spoon when you can ask for a 'cludthutter' instead?

279 **Have a go at snorkelling in the bath!**

277 Wear your clothes back-to-front for the entire day.

280 Put on every item of clothes you own, one on top of the other. Can you fit through the doorway wearing 23 t-shirts?

281 Go stair sledging. Wriggle into an old sleeping bag then slide down the stairs, shouting for your folks to get out of the way fast!

Woahh...

ONE-MINUTE MADNESS

Has anyone ever told you that you're very, very silly? They will after this lot!

282 Try to make yourself cry like a baby.

283 Give yourself a wedgie.

284 Pretend your bed is a monster then battle it into submission.

285 Watch tv with your eyes closed.

286 Perfect the art of raising one eyebrow, just like James Bond.

287 Pretend to lose your voice. Speak in a raspy whisper and write messages on a tiny notepad whenever you need something.

288 Make up a poem using the words 'slug', 'duster' and 'T. rex'.

289 Send a letter to a leading politician calling for him or her to back a nationwide campaign against nagging, broccoli and homework.

290 When your mum next tells you to be as quiet as a mouse, give it a go. Sit in silence for as long as you can, timing yourself with a stopwatch. Coughs and sniffs count as noises - start again!

SILLY SCORE

291 Get belching
Sure it's rude, but it doesn't count when you're out of earshot. Can you increase the volume and length of your belches or even burp the alphabet?

293 Get married to yourself
Make sure it's a beautiful ceremony, give thank you speeches and talk about what a lucky guy or gal you are to have found... yourself!

292 Become a D.I.Y. rock god. Raid the kitchen utensils and headbang in your room. Can you twirl your 'sticks' and thrash the air guitar?

294 Try humming the theme tunes to as many tv shows as you can in 10 minutes.

BEHIND CLOSED DOORS

295 Become a human chameleon. Dress in the right colour clothes to match your hiding place then lie there until someone comes in. Lay as still as a statue before surprising them with a massive **BOO!**

296 **Hop around the house for an entire day. Pointless, but funny.**

297 Practice ballroom dancing with your largest soft toy as a partner. Tape their arms and legs to yours and try out your most flamboyant moves. Can you fandango with a stuffed giraffe or cha cha cha with a cuddly cat?

ANIMAL CAPERS

298 Make leads for your stuffed animals then take them round the house for a walk.

299 Turn into Batman
Make a circle with your thumb and forefinger on each hand, with the other fingers pointing upwards. Rotate your hands then place the circles so they are like glasses against your eyes, with your palms resting against your face and your fingers pointing down along your jaw line. **The caped crusader has entered the building!**

MIGHTY MESSY

300 Face paint yourself without a mirror. Go for the boldest designs and colours you can think of. Now march into your little sister's bedroom and take a seat at her dressing table. What do you look like?!

301 Make up a musical based around the story of your life so far.

302 Parents calling you down for dinner? Button yourself inside your duvet or quilt cover, lie very still and see how long it takes for anyone to find you.

303 Create a glass orchestra. You'll need eight wine glasses filled to different levels. Dip your forefinger in the water and start to make circles round the rim of the first glass. Don't take your finger off, and when it starts to get dry you'll get a note. Now see if you can play a tune.

304 Next time mum asks you to clean up your bedroom, wind sticky tape, sticky side out, all round your hands. Now go around your room wiping your taped hands across the furniture to collect as much dust as possible!

EVERYBODY... NEEDS A BODY

305 **Paint a picture with your foot.**

306 Do everything with the wrong hand for the day. If you're left-handed, use only your right and vice versa. How much longer does everything take you and what sort of state is your homework in?

307 **Take up bum-walking**
Sit on your bottom with your legs in front of you and your arms crossed, then walk using only your bottom!

308 Make up your own crazy yoga position. What's the weirdest pose you can get your body into?

309 Skip everywhere, only stopping to burst into song like a character from your fave musical. Not only will you be keeping fit, your good mood will irritate your folks beyond belief!

310 Create some body art. Strip down to your oldest underwear, cover your body with water-based paint, then roll around on some blank paper.

SILLY SCORE

311 Give your face a work-out - it's funniest with a mirror. Stretch your mouth into the widest O possible then draw it into a little O. Roll your eyes upwards and raise your eyebrows. Now drop your features into a frown. Stick your tongue out as far as possible, then move it into a circle - can you touch your nose?

312 Choreograph your own OTT dance routine and get your family to give you a score. Find an upbeat chart hit, then work out a dance routine that makes full use of the space in your sitting room. Roll around on the rug, hip-shake past the telly, boogie by the bookshelf then throw yourself onto the sofa in a breathtaking finale.

313 Find out how double-jointed you are. Put your palms flat on a table and see if you can move your wrists to a right angle.

PARENT ALERT!

314 Can you fart at will? Hone your windy skills and you'll never need a whoopee cushion again. If your folks get mad tell them that in France it's an art form called La Petomanie. They'll be totally impressed with your linguistic prowess.

315 Make hammocks for your toys using your mum's bras.

316 Prepare an Oscar winner's speech. Make sure you sniff and snivel while thanking your granny for taking you to the movies.

317 Snip 'HI DAD' out of every other page of your dad's newspaper before he has the chance to read it.

TOP PRANK

318 Turn yourself into a mermaid or a merman. Put both of your legs into one pyjama leg and tuck the other up into the waistband. Mermaids can also raid their mum's underwear drawer for a bra or bikini top. Now flap around dramatically shouting for people to get you to water.

ONE-MINUTE MADNESS

Just when you thought they couldn't get any more stupid...

319 Gargle your country's national anthem with a cup of water.

320 **Take pictures of other people's ears.**

321 Become a Star Trek Klingon. Grab a mirror and put your hand on your head so your fingers point towards your forehead, now push down as hard as you can. Your forehead will wrinkle into a Klingon frown.

322 **Give amateur yodelling a try.**

323 Make yourself a medal for the world record shortest time spent cleaning your teeth.

324 Be ridiculously nice and helpful to everyone for the day. See how long it takes before someone begs you to stop. They'll only have themselves to blame when you revert to your former behaviour.

325 **Create some Frankentoys!**
Rummage through your toy box and pull out the broken body parts of your old playthings. Form new creations, tying bits together with shoe laces. Now leave the gruesome creatures round the house in unexpected and weird places.

326 **Take up rhythmic gymnastics. Make your own stick and ribbon and see how many patterns you can make in the air. Now grab the old hula hoop from the garage and start swinging across the front lawn. It'll keep the neighbours amused!**

BEHIND CLOSED DOORS

BEHIND CLOSED DOORS

327 Run a marathon on the spot. It'll take training – you'll need to jog for four to five hours. Why not collect sponsorship from your relatives? You could even suggest your own worthy cause, such as the 'Mike needs a new bike fund' or 'Sarah's laptop challenge'.

328 Try talking in a different regional accent for the day.

329 Play basketball in bed! Stick a plant pot on your bookshelf then see how many 'hoops' you can score using soft balls and rolled up socks.

330 Try speed-dating your dolls and action figures – will love blossom between Barbie and the Blue Power Ranger?

331 Do a sightseeing tour round your house. Stop at the most historic or unusual 'sights' and have a good gawp. Use your mobile to photograph the natives in their natural habitat – mum in the bath, dad snoring in front of the TV...

332 Take a star turn and give yourself a celebrity makeover. Choose your favourite TV or movie character or actor and actress. Make yourself look as much like them as possible using clothes, hairstyling and make up. See if your friends and family can guess who you're supposed to be.

333 Boost your self-confidence by walking over hot coals! Make your own 'coals' by colouring paper orange and red, scrunching the sheets up and placing them in a wide strip. Now try running over them while making authentic 'oooh' and 'aahh' noises. Award points for the quickest completion time.

334 How many of you? Google yourself to see how many of you there are in the world. Now pretend to assume one of your identities - maybe you're a respected French scientist or a beekeeper from Brazil.

335 Find out how electric you are. Blow up several balloons then charge them up by rubbing them repeatedly on your hair. Now see how many you can stick to the walls!

336 Practice taking your underpants off without removing your trousers. It can be done, but the trick is to wear very loose trousers.

BEHIND CLOSED DOORS

337 Make a mix-tape message. Pull out interesting song lines from your favourite CDs then edit them to make a message or letter for a friend.

WARNING: WACKY WIND-UP!

338 Rearrange all the soft furnishings in your house. Put cushions, throws, bedspreads onto the wrong beds and sofas. This one's satisfyingly simply, but it's guaranteed to drive your mum completely and utterly bonkers!

339 Perfect the art of plate-spinning. All you need is the handle of a feather duster and some plastic picnic plates. It might take a while to learn, but think how impressed your mates will be when you manage to pull it off!

What did you say...?

340 Have an intense and serious phone call with yourself or an imaginary best friend.

MUST BE MAGIC

Abracadabra, kalamazoo! Are you ready to amaze and astound your friends and family with your magical prowess? This chapter features a host of **tricks** and **illusions** so jaw-dropping they'd make Houdini look like an amateur. Turn the page then transform yourself into a **brilliant** but barmy **magician!**

341 To do magic you're going to need a wand. Make your own using black card rolled into a tube with two white strips of paper taped in place at either end.

Hey presto!

342 Wow your pals and frighten your folks with this tablecloth trick – whip a cloth off a laid table without smashing the crockery! To pull it off, make sure that the cloth doesn't have any wrinkles. Place any plates or cutlery near the edge of the table and then grab both corners of the cloth and pull it downwards rather than towards you. To begin with probably best to use plastic crockery!

343 Show your strength by performing a spoon-bending feat! Hold a metal spoon with the tip pointing down towards a table, covering up the handle with both fists. Pretend to push the spoon down onto the table, then secretly angle the spoon back towards you so that it appears to be bending. Ham up your acting, keep everything hidden with your fists and your pals will be begging for more!

344 Make the most of mirror magic for this quick trick. Balance a mirror against a piece of furniture, put one leg over it and lift it off the floor a little. When people look in the mirror you'll appear to be floating above the ground!

345 **Magic Circle refuse to admit you? Start your own society of kid magicians then start swapping tips and tricks. Be very shifty and secretive at all times.**

Silly secret

346 **Cover a glass paperweight with a silk scarf, then invite your family to step into your bedroom to have their fortunes told. Peer into the glass and shake your head, tut and look worried. Refuse to reveal anything until your palm is filled with silver.**

I can see into your future . . .

347 ### Learn to levitate!
Stand two metres away from your spectators. Turn to the side so that your left foot is sideways to the audience. Make sure that your left foot hides all of your right foot apart from the heel. Stick your arms out to the sides. Now keeping the left foot level, slowly lift yourself up on the ball of your right foot. To the audience you will appear to hover above the ground!

348 ## Top banana
Choose a ripe banana and poke a needle in about half way down. Rotate the needle inside the skin and you'll cut the banana in half without marking the peel. Repeat this from the opposite side. Leave the banana in the fruit bowl and when you're ready to amaze your folks pretend to cut it with an invisible knife before peeling it - the top will magically fall off!

349 You might have seen a jumping bean, but have you ever seen a prancing paper clip? Fold a bank note so that when you look down from above the edge forms an 'S' shape. Now attach the paper clips to close the S. One paperclip should attach the top to the middle bend of the 'S' shape. The other clip should attach the bottom to the middle bend. Slowly pull the ends of the bank note. The paper clips will slide as if by magic, coming together in the centre.

MUST BE MAGIC

MUST BE MAGIC

350 Slide a rubber band over your index and middle fingers. Secretly close your fist so that all four of your fingers are inside the rubber band. Show someone your closed fist and point to the two visible fingers that are under the rubber band. As you're pointing you say, 'The rubber band is on these two fingers, right?' Now open up your hand and bellow, 'Wrong!'

351 Brighten up a boring spelling test by showing your classmates this amazing rubber pencil trick! Hold a pencil near one end, then move your hand up and down fast. With a bit of practise it will look like the pencil is made of bendy rubber.

352 Create a mystical magician's outfit. Make a cape out of a towel then choose a knock-out hat. Will you plump for a wizard-style cone, a jaunty fez or a crazy sun hat borrowed from your gran?!

353 Shuffle a deck of cards and then have a sneaky look at the card at the bottom. Drop the cards from the bottom to the floor one by one and tell someone to say stop when you have got to about ten. Pick up the cards that you have dropped and pile them up again, making sure that you place the original card from the bottom of the deck back at the top of the pile. Show your friend this card, but do not show yourself and then get them to shuffle the pack. Now simply look through the deck and amaze them as you pick out the card that you looked at.

354 Next time you are served a bread roll throw it hard to the ground by your feet – it will magically bounce back up so you can catch it. The trick is to appear to throw it, but when your hand disappears behind the table create the sound of it hitting the floor by stamping your foot. This distracts people so you can turn your palm up and throw the roll up in the air again. Catch it and take a big bite!

355 Boil a glass of water without using a kettle or stove. Fill a glass with a little water, then angle it so the sun's rays point at the liquid. Hold a strong magnifying glass in front of the glass and keep still. The water will eventually boil!

ONE-MINUTE MADNESS
Each of these nippy tricks will be sure-fire hits...

356 Put three plastic cups upside-down on the floor, placing a ball under one. Mix the cups around then challenge your pals to find it every time.

357 Secretly stuff a clean tissue into your cheek then stun your little sis by pulling it out of your mouth when she comes into the room a few moments later!

358 Roll a piece of paper into a tube then look through one end, keeping both eyes open. Then hold your other hand up next to the tube. After a moment you'll see a big hole appear in your hand!

359 Appear to jam your finger through your ear by bending it away from your audience at the knuckle and simultaneously poking your tongue into the opposite cheek.

360 Pretend to break your nose! Put both palms facing each other over your nose. Hook one thumbnail under your front tooth. Make a gruesome grimace and pop your nail off your tooth to make an awful cracking noise as you bend your nose.

361 Read an adult's mind, by just asking them to follow these instructions:

1: Think of a country that starts with the letter D.

2: Now take the last letter of that country and think of an animal that jumps that starts with that letter.

3: Now take the last letter of that animal and think of a colour that starts with the same letter.

Now place your hand on the grown-up's forehead then close your eyes...

You: You're thinking of an orange kangaroo in Denmark!

The adult's eyes will pop out in amazement!

363 Make your own magic dust! Pocket handfuls of glitter or silver shaped confetti and sprinkle it liberally as you do your tricks.

362 Sign your sis or a friend up as a magician's assistant! Give them a name like 'Debbie', 'Sharonika' or 'Lulu'. To be a successful sidekick they'll need to wear skimpy clothes, daub themselves in bad make-up and pose a lot!

364 As a magician you're gonna need a rabbit! Dress one of your sister's favourite dolls up as a bunny or try to persuade your dad to stick on a cottontail and cute ears, then jump out from behind the sofa as your final trick.

MUST BE MAGIC

365 Put a glass of water on the table and cover it with a hat. Bet your friend that you can drink the water without touching the hat. He'll chuckle when you go under the table and start make drinking noises as if you're somehow sucking the glass from below. After a few seconds, come out, sit down and wipe your mouth. Your friend will remove the hat to see if you've succeeded. Now grab the glass of water and drink it. You've won the bet!

366 Are you a wannabe Houdini? Take turns tying each other up with the cord of your dad's dressing gown. Which one of you can escape in the quickest time?

367 'Abracadabra' is so last century! Make up your own brand new magical command.

TOP PRANK

368 Fake your own kidnap! Poke your head round the edge of a doorway so that your body is hidden from view. Hold the edge of the door with one hand and keep the other out of view, then talk to whoever is in the room. Suddenly bring your other hand up, grab your head and yank it out of sight. Cry for help!

369 **Got long hair?** Next time you're chewing some gum take a strand of hair (that is still attached to your head) and stick the end into the gum. Chew away for a while then spit the gum out and flick your head to the left. The gum should swing all the way round your head and back into your mouth, making onlookers think that it has flown by itself!

MUST BE MAGIC

Kerrrrching!!! Money Magic

370 Catch coins off your elbow! Put your arm straight out in front of you, palm down, then bend it at the elbow so that your palm is up by your shoulder. Place a coin on your forearm then flick your arm forward and try to catch the dosh!

371 Next time your dad dishes out your pocket money, make it disappear into thin air! Place a coin on the back of your hand then form a fist. With your leading hand click your fingers above the coin again and again. Keep getting closer until the clicking finger actually makes contact with the coin and flicks it up your sleeve.

372 Transform your bedroom into a magic emporium. Pull the curtains, play strange classical music and turn the lights down low. Wrap yourself in a cape and charge intrigued guests a fee to step inside!

373 Beg your mum to take you to the toy shop. How quickly can you make your pocket money disappear?!

374 Wrap a rubber band around your fingers and thumb. Invite a friend to watch as you place a hankie in the hand that has the rubber band on it then turn your palm so it is facing up. With your other hand place a coin into the hankie and grip the coin from the other side with your fingers. Let the rubber band slide off your fingers and wrap around the hankie and the coin. Give it a shake - it will seem as if the coin has vanished!

375 Funny money
This coin trick takes practise, but get it right and your mates will be talking about your conjuring skills for weeks! Place a blank index card on top of a cup. Now put a coin on top of the card. If you flick the index card just right it will fly away, making the coin fall into the cup!

GROSS OUT

376 Show your friends a shiny new coin. Now pretend to toss it high into the air, fake swallow it, make strange faces as you pretend to digest it, then reach around behind yourself with the hand that still holds the coin and pretend to pull it out of your rear end.

Yuk!

377 Use sticky putty to press two coins of the same value together, heads facing out. As long as you bet heads, you'll always win the toss!

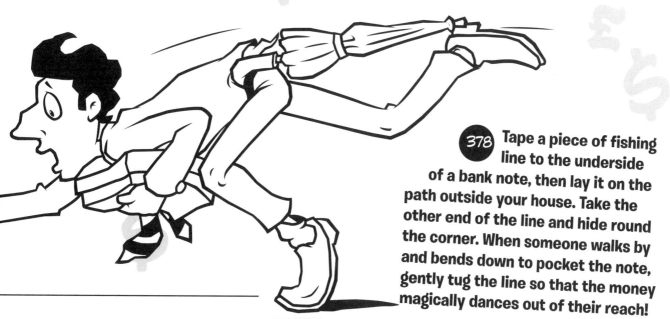

378 Tape a piece of fishing line to the underside of a bank note, then lay it on the path outside your house. Take the other end of the line and hide round the corner. When someone walks by and bends down to pocket the note, gently tug the line so that the money magically dances out of their reach!

379 Make your own magic potions! Stir up crazy shades using food colouring then add fizz for bubbles.

380 Hand your big brother a playing card, then place an A4 sheet of paper at his feet. Ask him to drop the card onto the paper – he'll find it impossible! Now earn his admiration by holding the card flat and parallel to the ground before dropping it – it'll land perfectly!

382 Camcord your head swivelling 360°!
Get a friend to film you swivelling your head slowly from side-to-side several times then stop recording. Take off your top and put it on back-to-front. Film yourself again moving your head from side-to-side. If you edit the film carefully it will look as if your head is turning all the way round!

381 Hold a small plastic cup, then place two dice between the cup and your thumb. Lift the cup up into the air and release one of the dice and catch it in the cup. Can you lift the cup up into the air and release the other die and catch it so that both dice are in the cup?

383 Static electrickery

Hold a biro vertically with the tip pointing upwards. Now dangle the lid above the tip of the pen. Squeeze with both fingers hard and the lid should shoot downwards and settle on the pen tip.

385 Your dad will be aghast when you show that you can balance coins on the end of a coat hanger. Bend a wire hanger into a diamond shape and hook it on your index finger so it hangs upside down. Balance a large coin on the tip of the hanging hook. Slowly rock the hanger back and forth, then go for a full circle – the coin should stay in place!

386 Secretly put a grape in your mouth, but don't swallow it. Put another grape in your left hand with its stem pinched between your fingers. Pretend to pass the grape to your other hand then pretend to smash the grape into your forehead. Now spit the first grape out of your mouth.

384 Need a crowd-pleaser? Pretend to stick a pencil in your ear! Hold a pencil at one end then lift the other end up to the side of your head. Now slide the pencil through your hand and up your arm. To your audience it will look as if the pencil is getting shorter because it's entering your ear, even though your hand and arm are simply hiding it from view.

TOP PRANK

387 Break your own neck! Hide a small empty plastic water bottle under your armpit. Call your audience in then proceed to jerk your head around with both hands, explaining that you've been suffering from neck ache for some time. When your head is at a very odd and painful-looking angle, crush the bottle under your arm so that it makes a horrific cracking sound!

MUST BE MAGIC

87

388 Compose your own magic spell. Skip round the house searching for ingredients. Gather the leg of a chicken, the eye of a needle, and some pond weed, then sing an enchanted rhyme to make your little brother less annoying.

389 When you're next out at a fancy restaurant, bet everyone that you can make the salt cellar lean over. Pour a pile of salt on the table and then gently lean the shaker up against it. Carefully blow the excess salt away and the salt jar should stay in its tilted position. Amazing!

390 Create your own magician's name - try rearranging the letters in your own name and adding 'The Great' or 'Mr' in front of them.

YOU MUST BE JOKING!

391 Surely only a very powerful magician could inflate their own head?! Pull on a baseball cap back-to-front. Sit on the sofa, put your thumb in your mouth and start to blow. At the same time lean back so that the peak of the cap pushes against the sofa, making it lift up as if your head has expanded in size.

392 Can you get a cork out of an empty wine bottle without breaking the bottle? Get a plastic bag and fold it into a thin strip lengthways. Push one end of the bag into the bottle, leaving the open end outside. Wiggle the plastic so the bit inside the bottle traps the cork at the top near the opening, then blow into the bag so the part inside inflates. Pull hard on the section hanging out of the bottleneck and the inflated bag will force the cork to come out!

393 Escapology for beginners...
Get your friend to button you into your coat back-to-front with the arms tied in a knot behind. See if you can get the coat back round the right way, untie the sleeves, slip them on and undo the buttons in under a minute.

394 Pretend to poke yourself in the eye with your finger, hooking it behind your eyeball. Suddenly screw your eye shut and scream out 'call an ambulance, I'm blind!'

MUST BE MAGIC

395 Try Voodoo spirit writing! You'll need a pad and a pencil and also a small piece of pencil lead taped to the inside of your thumb. Pretend to write on a piece of paper, but refuse to show your friend what you've scrawled. Now ask your pal to think of a shape and say the word out loud. While she's saying it, discreetly write her words down on the paper using the lead taped onto your thumb. When you show her the paper she'll be totally freaked.

396 Raid the kitchen when no one's around and make your mum's chocolate cake disappear as if by magic!

397 Small kids love marble magic. Show a littl'un a marble, put your hands together and blow, then let the marble roll down your sleeve. Show your empty hands to your audience. Pretend you can hear it flying around in the air and while your audience is distracted let the marble roll back into your hand! Astound your fan by plucking it from your ear.

398 Fill a glass with lemonade, then drop a plastic noticeboard pin into the liquid. Tell your friends that you are going to perform an ancient Indian ritual. Sway above the glass, muttering an incoherent chant. The pin will suddenly rise back up to the surface! Remember to take a bow. (The pin actually rises because the fizz bubbles stick to the plastic!)

399 **Crazy cup**
Stick a plastic cup to your thumb using a small bit of warm wax. Now move your thumb away from the cup slightly so that it is not noticeable that it's actually fixed in place. When you wiggle your thumb and fingers, it will look as if the cup is dancing about with the motion of your hand.

WARNING: WACKY WIND-UP!

400 Ask a buddy to write a name down on a piece of paper without you watching, then bet them that you have the exact same thing written on the piece of paper in your pocket. Get them to show you their paper. Now pull out the paper from your pocket on which you'll already have written the words 'the exact same thing'. **Gotcha!**

401 Make your mate float through the air! Ask a willing assistant to lie on their back, then drape a blanket over their body. While you're doing this they need to secretly roll over so that the audience doesn't realise that they're now lying on their front. Hover your hands above your pal and they should push their body up using both arms and the toe of one foot. The other leg should be lifted straight behind them so that their body looks like a plank. The moment you click your fingers they should collapse back to the floor.

GIGGLESOME GAMES

Games are the **ultimate** boredom busters! If you've lost the cash from your Monopoly set, the ace from your pack of cards and the dice from Snakes and Ladders - **don't panic!** All the challenges in this chapter simply need a silly sense of humour, a few willing chums and your spare time. Get set for some of the daftest matches around - **ready, steady, go!**

402 **Set up a woof-cam! Tape a video camera to your lower leg then walk round the house to get Rover's eye view of your family.**

SILLY SCORE

403 **Play Hopstar** - hopscotch in the style of a well-known Hollywood star. Your friends have to guess who you are. Their score is the number of the square you are on when they guess correctly.

404 Marbles are marbellous fun! Give yourself and a pal eight marbles apiece. Stand with your heels together and toes apart, then tell your friend to try and fling a marble into the space between your feet. If it gets there your mate keeps it. If it rolls out of the foot zone, it's yours for the taking. He who gets all the marbles, wins.

405 **Able to be a table?** Grab four chairs and five people. Arrange the chairs in a square with the seats facing inwards. Four of you should sit sideways on a chair with their legs swung to the right. Lean back so your heads rest on the thighs of the person to the left. When you're all in place, tell the fifth person to remove the chairs. This crazy stunt will amaze you!!

PARENT ALERT!

406 **Take your water pistol into the bath then practise shooting your mum's shower cap off the shelf!**

407 Scrunch up newspaper pages to make a stack of 'balls'. Each team takes a corner of the room. On the word 'go!' start the timer. Each team must throw balls out of their area into the other team's areas until four minutes is up. The team with the fewest balls remaining wins the match.

GIGGLESOME GAMES

408 Draw a flag or coat of arms that represents you. Are you a fan of football and ice cream, or perhaps a ballet dancer with a liking for thumb-wrestling? When you've finished sketching, mix up the papers and try to guess whose crest is whose.

410 Write the names of five people you would love to interview on strips of paper - maybe it's Britney, the Jonas Brothers or even the Queen of England. Pick a strip each then take turns being an interviewer or interviewee. Go on, ask whatever you like... does a servant really wipe the royal behind?

411 Hold a Handbag Auction. One person writes down a list of ten items that are in their (pretend) handbag, while the others have two minutes to write down what they think is inside. The winner is the person with the most matches.

409 **'All Hands On Deck'** gives players a great excuse to run about like nutters! Choose a **'captain'** to shout instructions to the group. **'Hard a-starboard'** means everyone must run to the right wall, **'hard a-port'** means sprint left, **'bow'** means go to the wall in front, while **'stern'** sends sailors to the back of the room. The last one to reach the wall each time is a land-lubbing loooooser!

412 Race your dad's undies! Cover a radio-controlled car with a shallow cardboard box so that the vehicle is almost entirely hidden, then secure it with sticky tape. Now snoop in your dad's drawer and pull out a crusty pair of pants. Drape the undies over the box to hide the cardboard. Ta-da! Radio-controlled pants!

GIGGLESOME GAMES

413 Try this daft version of 'Simon says'. The caller starts things off by shouting out the names of flying animals. With each call, the other players must flap their arms like wings. This should continue as the caller lists flying birds and animals, until the moment that they refer to a flock of non-flying creatures such as 'flying pigs'. The last person to stop flapping their arms is out.

414 Play noisy hunt the thimble! Hide a small object in the house and get your friends to find it. Give them clues by clapping harder and faster as they get near it and slower and lighter if they move further away.

415 Split into pairs then blindfold one person. The 'seeing' person must direct the 'blind' person around the room or house without them bumping into the sofa or the kitchen table!

416 Set up an obstacle course like a sock slalom or arrange chairs to crawl under and over. Now have an egg and spoon race! (If you don't want to get it in the neck from your mum, hardboil 'em first!)

417 **Up close and fruity!** Try passing an orange or apple along a line of mates without dropping it. You gotta pass the fruit from person to person under your chin and have your hands behind your back the whole time.

418 Sit down with your muckiest mate and brainstorm as many gross words as you can. Being vulgar is the name of the game here - 'barf', 'burp' 'puke', 'fart', 'poo' are all spot on! Write each word twice on separate pieces of paper. Now divide them up for a game of stinky snap.

GROSS OUT

419 Burp baby, burp! Get some mushy food like apple sauce and cups of fizzy pop. Divide into two teams. Each team should choose one nanny – the others become babies. Nannies must feed their babies a bowl of 'baby food' and wash it down with a fizzy drink. The babies have to sit on their hands at all times. The winning nanny is the person who gets all their babies to burp.

420 Have a crack at Wink Murder. Choose someone to be the 'detective' and send them out of the room while the rest of the group sit in a circle and decide who will be the 'murderer'. The detective should then sit in the middle of the circle while the murderer begins killing victims by winking at them. Can the detective work out who's the murderer before it's too late?

421 Ever noticed that yawns are catching? Start a chain off – and see if you can get your pet yawning, too.

GIGGLESOME GAMES

95

GIGGLESOME GAMES

422 Have a laugh playing Squeak Piggy Squeak. You'll need to find enough chairs for everyone minus one player. Once that player is blindfolded mix yourselves up and pounce on a chair. The blindfolded person must sit on every person's lap, working out who they are just by listening to their 'squeaks'. Can they suss each piggy in under two guesses?

423 Become Tom and Jerry for the morning. Half of you decide to be cats, the other half mice. Now go! Do whatever comes natural to your moggy or mousey natures.

424 Can you set a world record for something really silly? Try holding the most mushrooms or pulling off the longest animal impersonation.

425 Go teddy sledging Decorate a shoebox and attach a piece of string to the front through a hole. Stick your favourite stuffed toy inside and prepare to race! Watch out for ramming moves on the bends and pile-ups in the hallway!

DOUBLE DARE

426 Bored of board games? Up the ante with a forfeit or two! Next time you sit down to play Ludo, think up a rib-tickling dare for the loser. Maybe they've got to kiss a bald man on the head or do a comedy walk across the front garden? Every throw of the dice will become so much more thrilling as a result!

427 Try making up your own bizarre headlines using words cut from the newspapers. How about 'David Beckham eats Barack Obama's dog' or 'Britney Spears stole my slippers'.

428 Ask your pal to think of a person, place or object. You now have 20 questions to guess what it is! Your friend is only allowed to answer 'yes' or 'no'.

429 Run out of things to say? Find a piece of paper each, then draw a nutty body part. When you're finished, fold the paper down and pass it down the line. Start with the head, then add in the body, arms, legs and feet, passing it on at every stage. Open it at the end and meet your crazy characters!

YOU MUST BE JOKING!

430 Crack yourselves up with Wacky Who Dunnit. Get everyone to write down something daft that they've done. Perhaps you once tried eating a dog biscuit or went to school with your skirt tucked into your pants? Mix the papers up and deal them out, then try to guess who did what.

GIGGLESOME GAMES

LAUGHS BEFORE BEDTIME...

431 Pick a classic tale such as Little Red Riding Hood. Next choose a style – maybe romance, adventure or crime. Rope in your audience, then recount the story in that style.

432 Creep yourself out at the end of the day with a game of shadow monsters! Point a lamp towards a blank wall, then use your hands to create the shapes of the most fearsome beasts you can muster. No peeping under the bed once the light's turned out!

WEIRD OR WHAT?

433 How long would Snow White and the Seven Dwarfs last if the Ugly Sisters started bossing them around? Create your own gruesome fairy tale by writing all your favourite bits from one story together on sheets of paper and switching the sequences around. Who says you have to have a happy ending?

434 **Which one of you's the hairy godmother?**
Take turns acting out a mini-panto featuring your favourite bedtime story, then give each other marks out of ten for originality and comedy value.

435 Play Giants, Wizards, Elves – the extreme version of rock, paper, scissors! Giants must stand on their toes and growl menacingly; wizards wave their fingers and shout magical words; elves crouch down to the ground, and make high-pitched screeches. Giants squash elves, elves outrun wizards, and wizards stupefy giants.

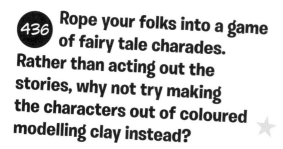

436 Rope your folks into a game of fairy tale charades. Rather than acting out the stories, why not try making the characters out of coloured modelling clay instead?

437 Get a carton of fresh eggs and place them along the ground outside. Show the eggs to a gullible pal, then tell him the story of the Golden Goose. Explain to your friend that you're going to blindfold him and lead him through the eggs, challenging him to sense which one might be golden. Once he's blindfolded, secretly replace each of the eggs with a small mound of dry cornflakes or gooey jelly. He'll get the shock of his life when he comes back and steps on each of the 'eggs'!

Silly secret

GIGGLESOME GAMES

ONE-MINUTE MADNESS

If you can find more contestants as a daft as you, this lot are gaming gold.

GIGGLESOME GAMES

438 Have a coin-flipping contest! Time each other flipping until you get either five heads or five tails in a row.

439 Blow raspberries instead of singing a popular song and see if the others can guess it.

440 Take turns to think up a word and write it in the air with your bottom, asking your pals to spell it out.

441 Play the Erm game. Time each other talking for a minute, without saying 'er' or 'erm'. If you do, play passes to the next person.

442 Practise 'shaving' each other. Use cans of whipped cream (the squirty kind) and see if you can perform a shave using a spoon.

443 Are you up for the thrill of Sharky Sharky? One of you plays the shark, stalking hungrily through the house. The other 'fish' scamper after you chanting 'Sharky Sharky, what's the time?'. The shark calls out random times until he fancies a snack. He then suddenly roars 'time for a bite!' and runs after the fish. The winner is the last fish swimming!

444 If there's a big crew of you, have a game of Superlatives. Split into two teams and choose one person to be the caller. Every time the caller shouts out a category such as birth months, height, or shoe size, the teams must arrange themselves into a line, starting with the smallest or first and going right through to the biggest or last in the sequence.

445 Get into pairs then race with balloons wedged between your bodies. Can you make it to the finish without an explosion?

446 **Who says party games are for babies? Have a hoot playing Musical Bundles! Dance around until the music stops, then throw yourself into a pile. Try to get as near to the bottom as you can – the person on top is out.**

447 Rope a load of mates into playing **Hectic Henhouse.** Form the henhouse by sitting everyone in a circle. A 'fox' should now walk slowly round the outside, patting each person on the head and saying 'hen'. When the fox pats someone and says 'goose' the person must jump up and both the goose and the fox run round the circle in opposite directions, trying to be the first to get back to the goose's place. The loser turns into the fox.

448 Ask your friends to write down an event on a piece of paper. It could be World War II, Christmas Day or Super Bowl Sunday. Once everyone has written something down, the papers are put in a bag, and the players are divided into two teams. A member of one team then chooses a piece of paper from the bag and has to act it out for their team to guess within two minutes.

449 **Invent a new card game with your own set of rules. How about a version of Old Maid that's set against the clock or a Snap game where the players have to shout a tongue twister every time the cards match up?**

450 Fancy some high pressure dressing-up? Gather two piles of grown-up clothing and two teams. Each team member has to get fully dressed up and race to the other end of the room and back, before giving their clothes to the next team mate to put on.

GIGGLESOME GAMES

GIGGLESOME GAMES

451 Form a line to make-up a Chinese dragon – the person at the front forms the head, while the last in the line pretends to be the tail. When you're ready to go, the head must try to chase and catch the tail. If the tail person gets caught they drop out and the dragon becomes shorter.

ANIMAL CAPERS

452 If your footie team's been knocked out of the cup or mum's serving Brussels sprouts for dinner, have a game of Crazy Cockerel to cheer yourself up! Choose a person to be the cockerel. They must cluck, strut and 'cockadoodle do' their way round the room in a chicken-like manner. Whoever chuckles becomes the next crowing cockerel, charged with making someone else laugh in order to rejoin the group.

453 Find some sticky reminder notes and play Celeb Head. Secretly write the name of a celebrity (alive or dead) on the note and stick it to the forehead of the person to your left. Now take it in turns to try to guess who you might be - questions can only be answered 'yes' or 'no'.

454 Invite your little sister to play Doctors and Nurses with you. Before she can protest truss up her dollies with loo roll and put lolly stick splints on her teddies.

455 Enemy Fire is a bonkers battle to have with your toughest mates! Grab some scatter cushions from the sofa then order one of you to run up and down the room. Everyone else must sit on the floor and become snipers. It's the snipers' job to take out their victim with cushions –

3, 2, 1, FIRE!

456 Make up super showbiz names. Take your first pet's name then add the first street that you lived in at the end. What will yours be?

THE NAME'S CREEK, ROVER CREEK

457 Write 20 emotions on scraps of paper such as 'happy', 'angry' or 'scared'. Put them in a pot, then take turns picking and acting out an emotion. Get ready to howl like a banshee or laugh like a lunatic... give marks for the best performance.

458 Release your inner kangaroo with Balloon Stomp! Blow up some balloons and then tie one to each of your friends' ankles. Now try and pop everyone's inflatables without getting your own balloon stomped on first.

459 Get your schoolmates ducking for cover in the playground by playing a soccer match using a rugby ball instead of a football!

460 Ready, bed-spready, go...

...for a drag race with a difference! Find some old bedspreads or towels, then share them out amongst your mates. Now pair up with a racing partner and take turns racing round the garden.

GIGGLESOME GAMES

461 Work out how old you are in dog years. One dog year is about the same as seven human years. When you turn eight, you'll actually become an a–paw–lingly ancient 56 years old!

462 Be the first to create an alien life-form with this fast and furious dice game. Take turns to throw a dice and draw the following alien body part on your paper for each of the numbers that you throw next: 1=body, 2=head, 3=antennae, 4=leg, 5=mouth, 6=eye. The winner is the first to complete a six-legged, four-eyed alien!

463 Wind a friend's body up in sticky tape - leave their neck and face free and one arm. Time how long it takes them to unravel themselves free!

465 Ask your mum to blindfold you and your friends, then spread pennies all across the floor. When she says 'go!', crawl around the carpet, picking up the cash. The richest kid wins!!!

WARNING: WACKY WIND-UP!

464 Share a room? Wait behind your bedroom door then ambush your little bro with a pillow. Give him the pillow fight of his life – you'll both be in stitches in seconds!

466 Freak yourself out with *TOUCH BOX*. Put some weird stuff in a small cardboard box. Try cotton wool, cubes of jelly, or perhaps a bumpy seashell. Blindfold your mates and give them a point for every item they get right, taking points away for any acts of wimpiness.

467 Set up a penguin relay. Find a soft toy or small ball. Place the object in between your knees and shuffle penguin-style across the room and back without dropping it. If you slip up, start again. Players must pass the item between their knees without using any hands.

AFTER DARK

Just think how much **mischief** you can get up to under the cover of **darkness!** Shine a torch on these pages and you'll see hilarious sleepover pranks, super-spooky games and enough crazy capers to keep you **laughing all night long.** No one else in your family will sleep easy again...

105

468 Get your mates' knees knocking with a game of **Hide and Scare.** When somebody finds you, jump out of your hiding place and let out a blood-curdling scream!

469 Mummify yourself! You'll need a roll or two of toilet paper and a friend to help you wind it round your body. When you're all tied up, walk around with your arms and legs outstretched, groaning eerily.

470 Make up spooky ghost stories using people and places you know – perhaps your old aunty Viv's run-down cottage or the empty building opposite your school with the boarded-up windows.

471 Dig out some old fashion dolls and give them a haircut and wardrobe makeover in the dark. Now flick on the lights to see the grim results.

472 **Backwards bedtime stories**
Share a room with a silly sister, bonkers brother or a twittish twin? Read each other to sleep, but start with the last page first.

473 **Dad fast asleep in front of the TV? Gently take off his socks and paint his toenails bright red!**

474 In the middle of the night, tiptoe into your little sister's room and turn all the posters upside down. She'll be totally freaked when she wakes up!

475 Play out a daft shadow Muppet show on the bedroom wall, starring the Cookie Monster, Miss Piggy and a shadow version of you!

476 Take a shower in the dark, but try not to muddle up the shampoo with mum's hair bleach!

477 Make yourself a cool eyeshade - use card to cut out a mask shape and then decorate it with freaky eyes or a message like **'buzz off'**.

ONE-MINUTE MADNESS
Snigger through the seconds with these daft light games!

478 Grab a torch, shine it up under your chin and make the most gruesome faces you can.

481 Chase each other's torch beams around the walls and ceilings.

479 Turn the lights on and off rapidly. Each time you flick the switch adopt a new crazy expression as if your face has been turned on and off too.

482 Blink wildly and then close your eyes really tight for an interesting light show.

480 Flick your torch backwards and forwards really fast, then get your friends to dance as if they are starring in an old black and white movie.

AFTER DARK

107

AFTER DARK

483 Turn all the lights off in your home and see how you'd manage in a sudden, prolonged power cut. Huddle round a candle, eat baked beans out of the can and bump into the walls.

484 See if you can snore loudly enough to drive your folks crazy! Score **5** points if they're in the room with you, **10** points if they storm in from another bedroom and **50** points if they're disturbed from watching TV in the living room downstairs.

485 Plot a midnight feast. Start squirrelling away biscuits, cakes and crisps for a few days before the banquet. If your mum notices you can always blame your little brother... or the dog.

486 Explore the great outdoors with a gloomy game of Torch Tag! One team sets off, each hiding in a separate place. The seeking team, armed with flashlights, embarks on busting each of their rivals' hiding places. Once spotted a hider must go to jail. The hiding team can rescue a jailed member if they get to them without being caught in a torch beam. When everyone is in jail, it is the other team's turn to hide.

YOU MUST BE JOKING!

487 Amaze your parents by telling them that you're getting ready for bed early tonight, then dress up in mum's frilly nightie or dad's sad stripy PJs. Now tuck yourself in... to their double bed.

488 Hang a sheet up in a darkened room or ask your tallest mates to hold the corners. Stand behind it concealing a torch and a water pistol. Get your friends to come in one at a time and kneel in front of the sheet. Tell them they must follow the torch beam across the sheet with their nose. When the torch beam (and their nose) gets to the edge of the sheet, squirt them! You'll be in fits as they jump around in surprise!

489 Try drawing yourself in the dark – mmm, don't you look abstract!

491 Freak the family out by waiting until dark then making a mini crop-circle on the front lawn!

490 Round up a group of mates in a pitch-dark room, close your eyes then try to guess who's who just by feeling each other's faces.

DOUBLE  **DARE**

492 Are you brave enough to play Horror Hide and Seek? After dark, turn out the lights and get one person to hide with a mobile phone. Start hunting the hider who must, every so often, call the home phone and give clues to where they are lurking.

AFTER DARK

AFTER DARK

493 Give Blackout Twister a spin. Getting all tied up in knots is so much funnier in the pitch black. Be careful where you put that hand!

494 Wait until your mum or dad falls fast asleep on the couch, then sneak up and dab a blob of shaving foam in their hand. Now go behind the sofa and tickle their nose with a feather or thread. You'll be in bits watching them scratch their nose with a hand full of cream!

495 Devise your own Morse code with torches and a series of long or short flickers. What rude words can you spell?

496 Play Eye Spy in a dark room, picking out objects with torches.

498 **Play catch. Sounds easy, but is soooooo much more difficult at night time!**

497 Grab all the pillows, sheets, duvets and bedding in the house and pile them up. Can you climb Quiltimanjaro?

499 Start a dream diary. Keep a notepad next to the bed, then scribble down your craziest dreams and freakiest nightmares. You'll be knocked out by your mind's mad imaginings!

GROSS OUT

500 Go on a torchlight safari to see how many mysterious beasties you can find hiding out in your garden. Tell your sister you've put a load of beasties in her bed!

501 Pull the curtains, then play Wizard of Darkness with your friends. Choose one person to stand in the middle of the room, then turn him round a few times until he gets disorientated. Now set him free and tell him to feel around in the dark until he touches someone. Every time he nabs a person, the wizard must guess by touching them who they are. If he guesses correctly, the person is recruited as an apprentice to join the wizard's team.

502 There's nothing scarier than a clown! Raid your big sister's make-up bag and smear a white eye shadow over your face. Put bright red lipstick on and around your lips and make two vivid circles on your cheeks. Now tiptoe over a sleeping pal and shake them awake. They will freak!

503 Dress up as aliens and stage an alien abduction.

504 Try night scouting. One of you must hide in the garden in the dark and then flash a beam of light for five seconds. Flick off the beam and see how long it takes everyone to find you.

505 Set up an obstacle course that goes around furniture and through rooms. Now try navigating it in the dark.

506 Doodle in the dark
Find some glow-in-the-dark markers then send secret messages to each other.

507 Strap a torch to your bicycle helmet and go on a night hike around the garden.

AFTER DARK

Silly Sleepovers

508 Smear petroleum jelly between a friend's toes to make them subconsciously wriggle all night.

509 Get some choccy biccies and put one on your forehead, chocolate side down. Put your hands behind your back, then try and wiggle the biscuit down your face and into your mouth!

510 Draw crazy facial hair on your sleeping pals.

511 Last one awake? Pull out a hair and gently stick it in someone's ear. See how many times you can do it before the person rouses and bats you away.

GROSS OUT

512 While your best mate is sleeping, gently put their fingers into a bowl of lukewarm water. In the morning they will have wet the bed! **Fact!**

513 If you wake up before it gets light, try starting a cat chorus in your neighbourhood. Open the window and then meow to the moon as loudly as you can. See if any local moggies howl back before your mum storms in to find out what's going on!

514 Flashlight limbo

Ask two mates to point torches towards each other to form a large beam for the rest of you to limbo under. Anyone breaking the beam is sent out of the dance line! Make sure that you move the torch light down after each round.

515 Set up a secret card school. Collect milk bottle tops or make a pile of Lego bricks, then share the stash out evenly with your friends. When the rest of the household are sleeping, sit in a circle playing card games. Gamble as many 'chips' as you dare, scanning your mates' faces for any signs of cheating!

516 Get all your guests to sling their pyjamas into the middle of the room, turn the lights off and then scrabble about getting dressed in the dark.

EEEK!!!

517 Squeezy sleep

Swap your quilt for a sleeping bag and find out how many of you can cram in it, or simply see how many mates can fit into your bed. Make sure no limbs are hanging out!

AFTER DARK

518 Climb into a duvet cover and point your hands into the far corners. Now blast out some classical music and perform a crazy modern dance around your bedroom.

519 Ratattack!
Attach a fake rat, mouse or other nocturnal animal to a string. Hide on one side of the doorway and when you hear someone coming, jerk the string to make the 'animal' dart across their path.

Eeeeeek!

520 Press a torch against your cheek and open your mouth. Your tongue and tonsils will glow a cool shade of science fiction red.

521 Wait till everyone's sleeping then blow softly on their face, neck, arms, hands or ankles.

522 Do a three-legged race around the house – with the lights off.

523 Turn off the lights then sit in a circle holding hands with your pals. The challenge ahead is quite simple - see who can sit in complete silence for the longest without cracking up! The person who chortles first is out.

524 Try making the hairs on your neck stand on end by thinking of the scariest teacher at school.

WEIRD OR WHAT?

525 Whistle a scary tune in the middle of the night – Thriller or the Jaws theme works well! If that doesn't freak out the folks, simply knock on the wall in a haunting manner.

526 Next time you have a friend over, shortsheet their bed. Tuck the bottom of the sheet in at the head of the bed and place the pillows on top. Fold back the rest of the sheet upwards from the centre of the bed so that it goes back up to the head of the bed and over the pillows. You then need to lay the duvet on top, turning the part of the sheet which went over the pillows down to cover the top bit of the duvet as normal.

528 Think up the silliest animal you can and imagine them jumping over a fence to try to soothe you off to sleep.

527 Need to get even with your big brother? Pull on a furry costume glove and hide under his bed. When he settles down for the night, make a loud monster roar, then reach up and grab his hand. Be ready to make a super-quick getaway afterwards!

529 ## Go clubbing!
If you don't have a disco ball, use torches and turn them on and off in time to the music. You could also wear glow-in-the-dark clothing to add extra atmosphere. Keep on boogying until your dad bangs on the living room ceiling!

AFTER DARK

Whooohoooo!

530 Hide in the garden and make some scary nocturnal noises. Howl like a wolf, screech like an owl or growl like a mythical monster.

531 Try guessing how many fingers and toes your best mate is holding up in the dark.

532 Hide in your parent's wardrobe then jump out at them when they come up to bed.

534 Whisper silly things into your dad's ear while he's asleep. The next morning ask him what he dreamt about – do they match your wacky whispers?!

533 Go crazy star-gazing. Don't worry if you don't know the Plough from Orion's Belt! Just lie on your back under a starry sky and pick out your own amazing or amusing shapes.

WARNING: WACKY WIND-UP!

535 Cause a bathroom brawl by replacing the family toothpaste with mayonnaise! Cut the end off a standard tube and squeeze out the paste. Now carefully fill it up again with mayo. When the tube is nice and plump, fold the end over as if it has been partially used. Tiptoe out and wait for your first victim!

536 Got a cat? Have fun watching Felix scamper round the room chasing the beam of light from a torch. He'll try to pounce and catch it, even if goes onto the ceiling.

FEELING CRAFTY?

Make it, cut it, stick it, glue it... it's time to roll up your sleeves and get your **hands dirty!** Forget flowery birthday cards and papier maché bunny rabbits - this guide is crammed with enough daft objects and homemade practical jokes to give your mum a total **'art attack!** Put on your oldest clothes and get crafty!

537 Make a cool family snapshot criminal-style. Take a full-length photo of each person from the same distance and cut them out of the background. Draw horizontal lines across a piece of white paper, writing heights at the edge of the lines. Now stick the photos down to make a line-up of family suspects.

538 Design an alternative book cover for your parent's favourite read, then swap yours for the real dust jacket and replace the book on their bedside table. Check out the hilarious titles at the top of each page for ideas!

539 Enjoy seeing your nearest and dearest portrayed as hardened jailbirds? Then make a registration board for each family member to hold up in their police mug shot. Write a convict number plus 'Los Angeles State Police Department' in chalk on a mini blackboard. Now ask your mum, dad or great-grandpa to hold it up when you take their picture!

YOU MUST BE JOKING!

540 See who can whip up the most original loo roll outfit in five minutes. Release the avant-garde designer in you - think turbans, sarongs, wrap-dresses and thigh-high boots.

541 Mallow Ammo

Give your irritating younger brother a pink and white pelting! You'll need marshmallows rolled in flour, a length of sticky tape and a clear plastic file wallet. Roll the wallet up from corner to corner to create a tube then tape it shut. Now insert your mallow bullet and blow hard to make it fly out at your target!

542 Create a junk sculpture in the middle of your living room. Collect old cereal boxes, empty cartons, fabric scraps and plastic bottles then start building. Make something as big and dramatic as you can.

543 Can't bear sharing a room with your pesky brother or sister? Make one room into two! Grab some masking tape and stick a single clear line down the centre of the room. If he or she steps onto your side... there'll be consequences.

WARNING: WACKY WIND-UP!

544 Get noticed in the school dinner hall. Drink down a juice carton then blow it back up using the straw. Place the inflated carton on the ground then stamp hard with your foot.

Ka-boom!

545 Create your own bumper stickers for your parents' car window. How about 'OUR OTHER CAR'S A TOY' or 'THESE PARENTS HAVEN'T PASSED THEIR DRIVING TEST'. Stick them onto the bumper with a load of sticky tape.

546 Tie your foreign coin collection on to the branches of your mum's fave house plant, then convince your baby sister that money really does grow on trees.

547 **Build a domino chain with books, CDs or any junk you can find that will stand on one end and fall when nudged.**

548 Make your own water slide! It's best to start with the kind of plastic sheeting builders use but you could also try taping several black bin liners together. Lay the slide on the lawn, then point a hosepipe on it so that the water streams along the plastic. Add some washing-up liquid for extra slippery, bubbly fun.

549 **Paint parts of your body then roll around on some white paper.**

550 **Feeling grouchy?**
Getting grief from your oldies about cheering up? Make yourself a happy mask! Get a brown paper bag hold it upside down then cut two eyeholes for you to see out of. Draw an enormous grin on the front in marker pen. Now you're free to frown and scowl as much as you like and it'll go completely undetected by everyone.

551 Get a friend to stretch a rubber band wide, then write a secret sentence along it. Once they let go the words will shrink down into gobbledygook. This is a great way to pass messages around the classroom!

silly secret

552 Create your own tattoos. Find some washable coloured pens then draw body art on yourself or your friends. Try your favourite soccer teams, cartoon characters and names – whatever floats your inky boat.

553 Make a paper boomerang out of brown cardboard. Draw an equal-sided cross on the card with each arm measuring eight centimetres long by three centimetres thick. Cut the cross out and give it a test spin across the garden.

554 Make a fake ID! Cut a photo of your head out and stick it on some card, then draw facial hair and a dodgy hair-do over the top. Cover the card with cling film or sticky back plastic. Put on dark glasses and turn up your collar and see how far you get before anyone recognises you...

555 Do some staple or hole punch art. You'll need to round up some paper, a staple gun and a hole puncher. Go crazy.

556 Parents too stingy or uptight to fork out for a mobile phone? Make your own telecommunication system using two empty tin cans and a long piece of string tied between them. OK it's primitive, and you may be restricted to chats with your little brother, but if your parents trip over the string enough times they may reconsider shelling out for the real thing.

ANIMAL CAPERS

557

Make a Paris Hilton style outfit for your dog you could use doll's clothes or toddler outfits - or put him in your t-shirt with the arms rolled up.

FEELING CRAFTY?

558 What if The Borrowers were real? Create a welcoming and homely environment for mini people in your bedroom just in case. Make cosy rooms out of cereal boxes, chairs out of cotton reels and stick funky gift-wrap on the walls.

559 **Sick of your parents holding the threat of Santa's naughty list over your head? Pre-empt them this year by making your own tiny stocking – use a baby sock or cut one out of paper and decorate it.**

560 Give full vent to your creative side by inventing a brand new musical instrument. Use scissors to cut the pointed tips from two wooden barbecue skewers. Thread 15 beads tightly together onto each tip and use glue to secure the beads at each end in place. When the glue is dry, play your instrument by rubbing the beaded sections against each other. Hey, funky!

561 **Welly dull?**
Fancy new gumboots? Open some bottles of craft paint, then brighten them up with go-faster stripes, googly eyes or slogans with attitude.

562 **Make trick dog poo!** You can be truly creative in order to get just the right consistency. Experiment with flour, water, salt, sugar, crumbled biscuits and peanut butter. When you've got your mixture ready either mould it into an authentic sausage shape or smear a runny doggy 'pat' onto your dad's shoe.

563 Get two bread rolls and two forks. Stick the forks into the bread rolls then do a little dance with your two bread feet.

TOP PRANK

564 Make a stunt leg! Cut the leg off an old pair of jeans from the knee down. Now take a sock and fill it with scrunched-up newspaper. Put the stuffed sock in a shoe or trainer and push the cut-off jean over the sock. When the time's right, leave your stunt leg poking out from under a car wheel, or have it hanging out of the boot.

DOUBLE DARE

565 Mould tiny egg shapes out of air-drying clay then squidge them onto a stick. Push in short bits of pipe cleaner for legs and paint the whole thing green. Add some googly eyes and you've created a bug army! Are you bold enough to leave your queue of critters on your teacher's desk?

566 Survive a fatal archer's blow. Cut an arrow shape out of some sturdy brown card then use red card to make a triangle for the pointed tip and feathered end. When your arrow looks convincing, cut it in half. Use sticky tape to fix one piece to one side of a plastic hair band and the other end to the other side. Pop it on your head and grimace.

FEELING CRAFTY?

567 Find two empty plastic bottles of the same size. Fill one three-quarters full with water and a couple of drops of food dye. Place the empty one on top neck down so the two open ends are together. Tape the necks of the two bottles together. Now swirl them round and watch what happens.

568 Caught without a toboggan in winter? A creative genius like you can soon solve that! Experiment with whatever household objects you can lay your hands on. Try large plastic refuse bags, dustbin lids and round dinner trays

569 Dig out two photos of the same size, but very different colours. Cut them into equal-sized vertical strips then glue them onto a piece of card. Alternate strips from one picture to the next and you'll get some hilarious results! This is side-splitting if you do it with similar-looking relatives.

FEELING CRAFTY?

teehee!

Pizza the action
570 Create a fake pizza then leave it in the fridge for your family. Cut a circle out of a piece of brown card and stick scrunched up newspaper around the edge for the crust. Cut out topping shapes such as pepperoni, strips of onion and mushrooms. Stick the card toppings on, then paint the pizza with a solution of PVA glue mixed with water. Before it dries cover the whole delicacy with tissue paper then paint your pizza in mouthwatering foody colours.

571 Create a fairy ring in some long grass at the bottom of your garden. Tramp down the grass to form a circle, make a set of card toadstools, then sit and wait for the magic folk to make an appearance.

572 Make your own bedroom door sign out of cardboard cut into a hook shape. Decorate it with stickers and a harsh warning to anyone who dares to step inside.

573 Find photos of your mates and paste them onto a large sheet of card in a crazy higgledy-piggledy way. The pics will look even better if they overlap. When you're done ask your mum to buy you a cheap clip frame to put it in.

MIGHTY MESSY

574 Do you love those chocolate eggs with a surprise inside? Keep the egg-like plastic containers and make a brand new fashion statement! Use a needle and cotton to thread the capsule halves together to form a cool necklace or chain.

575 Do a flour drawing. Cover the table with plain or self-raising flour then use a finger to create cool pictures or make a graffiti design. If you go wrong you can just start again!

FEELING CRAFTY?

125

ONE-MINUTE MADNESS

Who could fail to see your artistic talent after completing one of these minute makes?

576 Make your own fling ball out of a tennis ball and a sock. Put the ball into the end of the sock then use the other end to fling it to great heights.

577 Don't want to talk to your parents? Make a 3D Lego message for them.

578 Create own fridge stickers for your family using paper and felt-tip pens. Try 'YES MUM, YOUR BUM DOES LOOK BIG IN THAT' and 'STEER CLEAR, TOXIC BROCCOLI INSIDE'.

579 Make a tickle stick! Tape a feather duster to the end of a broom, then sit on the other side of the living room and annoy your siblings.

580 Create daft pencil toppers out of play dough, adding raisins for eyes and slivers of carrot for fangs.

FEELING CRAFTY?

581 Pastry Picasso
Create a tasty confectionary creature. Buy a round Danish pastry, then draw a lion's body on a sheet of paper and colour it in with pens. Simply position the pastry as the lion's head and add eyes, ears and a muzzle cut out of paper and coloured in. Grrrrab a plate and get scoffing!

582 Mix your own make-up! Use a piece of charcoal as an eyebrow pencil. Petroleum jelly with glitter stirred in makes great sparkly lip-gloss or you could go Elizabethan and pat your face with some sieved flour. It won't be pretty, but at least you'll be unique!

583 Make like Jackson Pollack and create a crazy abstract picture using squirty paints and household objects – no brushes allowed.

584 Make your own mood rings - you can buy really expensive ones with stones that change colour according to mood, but these mysterious changes are only due to shifts in body temperature. Make your own much more reliable ones out of paper decorated with happy, grumpy or serious faces. Wear and flash them as the mood takes you!

GROSS OUT

585 Want to skip school? Make some scary-looking pee. Start complaining of a tummy ache the night before you fancy a day off. On the morning go to the loo and carefully pour a few drops of either blue or red food colouring into the toilet bowl. Show your mum and wa-hey ~ 'urine' bed again before you know it.

586 Have a laugh with crazy hand hair. Get a photo of a loved one, cut out the face and neck (without their hair) and stick it onto a larger piece of card. Now paint your palms in crazy colours and print a rainbow afro using your hands and fingers.

587 Make some marshmallow men! All you need are some marshmallows, cocktail sticks and a pen to draw on funny facial expressions.

588 Create gnashers to make your dentist weep! Take an orange and cut it into large segments. Now score goofy teeth into the peel and cut out the rest of the peel. When you're ready to flash your gnashers, pop the segment into your mouth to create a corking dental make-under.

FEELING CRAFTY?

MONSTER MAYHEM

589 'Borrow' a rectangular tissue box from the sideboard, then carefully remove the tissues and keep them safe. Paint the box all over with acrylic paint in a bold, monstery colour. Cut two sections out of an egg box and paint them white, then glue them onto the top of the box to make eyes. Add a line of white card teeth around the tissue opening before sticking card claws and a tail onto the base. Put the tissues back in the box and leave it out in the living room. Will any snotty people dare to reach into the beast's mouth?

MIGHTY MESSY

590 Splat monsters are sooo much fun! Squirt paint randomly onto a large sheet of paper - the messier the better. Wait until the colour dries then add white circles of paper for eyes. Now draw on the pupils in black marker and add toothy grins. Cut out your creature shapes then stick them on your bedroom door.

591 Make some sick sock puppets. Stick bloodshot ping-pong ball eyes on a sports sock, then decorate it with red sticker spots and yellow boils. Add wool hair and a monstrous moustache to top off your hideous creations!

592 **Gruesome grass man!**
Cut the foot off a pair of old tights. Put a little grass seed in the end of the foot and fill it with sawdust. Tie the bundle up tightly, then turn it upside-down so the tied end is at the bottom. Sit your creation in the opening of a jam jar. Glue scary eyes, a nose and a toothy grimace onto the stuffed hosiery, then gently water it. Your monster will grow a shock of green hair within just a few days!

593 Grab your coat, go for an autumnal walk and collect some pine cones. Now turn them into crazy cone creatures – first paint them, then add felt ears, eyes, wings and fangs!

FEELING CRAFTY?

WARNING:
WACKY
WIND-UP!

594 Beastly bouquet...
Hunt down a florist's oasis block, some tissue paper and pipe cleaners. Put the oasis in a flowerpot, then decorate the pot with stickers. Wind layers of coloured tissue round the top of the pipe cleaners and secure them with tape to make flowers. Stick the stems into the oasis until you've created a lovely bunch of blooms. Now find your scariest plastic bug and pop it in the middle. Present it to mummy dearest and wait for the screams.

595 Ever reared tin foil tadpoles? Baby froglets are pretty boring till they grow legs, right? **Wrong!** Tadpoles are perfect for racing. Take two marbles and mould a rectangle of silver foil around each one, pinching the back to make a tail. Leave the bottom open so that the marble can spin inside the foil case, then get ready to watch 'em go!

596 Make your own wormery. Dig up a bunch of worms, then collect together a large glass jar, some soil and a few leaves. Add the worms, gently pack the soil on top then punch holes in the top of the container for air. With these slithery pets in residence your mum is far less likely to come knocking on your bedroom door!

PUTTING ON A SHOW

'Don't make a **scene**!', 'no **showing off**!', 'stop playing the **fool**!'. Do these phrases sound horribly familiar? If so, you're gonna love this chapter! It's stuffed full of silly one-liners, daft dancing and **crazy theatre craft**. So the next time that your oldies give you grief about showing off, tell them that Charlie Chaplin made a good living out of doing just that!

GROSS OUT

597 Give an under-arm fart concert. Dress up to the nines beforehand in your parents' black tie or evening gown. Looking very serious, sit down at the piano or with an instrument. Now ignore it completely and give a virtuoso performance using a cupped hand under your armpit. Squelch!

598 Grab some green gear then get ready for a crazy Irish river dance. This hilarious routine works best with fast folk music. Stand in a line-up and make yourselves as stiff as boards, clamping your arms to your sides. Now flick out your ankles in time to the beat. Try to throw in a few high kicks without falling over!

599 Ask your mum to tell you about her favourite movie love scene - she'll have loads 'cos she's a girl! Afterwards raid her wardrobe and make-up bag, then re-enact every swoon wearing her best dress and salmon-coloured lipstick. We're sure she'll be just as moved by your performance, not!

600 When you next sit down to watch TV, spice up the boring ads by acting out a few of your own! As soon as the commercials come on, mute the sound and reach for the nearest person. Start your spiel, grinning cheesily at your bewildered family. How about saying: 'For just 3.99 a month you could be the proud owner of this mumatron. It'll do all the washing, ironing and cleaning you need or your money back guaranteed!'

601 Stage a synchronized swimming show on your sitting room carpet. Stick a clothes peg on your nose, pull on your bathing gear then 'jump in' and make up some great splashy formations.

132

602 The wig wag

This is a hoot if you've got short hair! To make it work you'll need to rope in a girl with long locks. Put two chairs back-to-back with one facing your audience and one turned in the opposite direction. You should sit looking at the audience with the girl hidden behind. When you're both ready the girl should tip her head back so that her hair drapes over your head. Suddenly you've got a radical new hair do!

603 Learn your entire national anthem backwards, singing along to the same tune. Wait for an important sporting event and when your team step onto the pitch, stand up theatrically and perform your topsy-turvy tribute.

604 Surprise your pals with a shoe reading. Grab one of your mate's trainers then peer into the sole in a mystical way. Suddenly announce that you have a vision, saying 'I have seen the future... you will be going on a short trip'. Now fling the shoe as far as you can into the distance. Looks like their trip is coming sooner than they thought!

605 Slouch on the sofa and pull up your t-shirt so that your tummy's bare. Draw a pair of eyes and a nose on your torso, using the belly button as the mouth. To make belly man speak, pull the skin on either side so that your belly button changes shape. Insist on only communicating through belly man until you're ready to shift off the sofa.

606 Pop stars, you gotta love them, especially when they're writhing around on TV! Pick your favourite wacky clip and re-enact it in your bedroom – think Miley, Beyoncé and Kanye...

607 Act out a day in the life of your mum and dad. Think realism at all times, capturing your dad's swear words when he can't find clean socks in the morning and your mum's fury when she realises that your little brother has forgotten to do his homework yet again.

608 Follow in the graceful steps of Fred Astaire, a famous tap-dancer with flying feet. Do your own tribute on a tiled floor. If you can't borrow some tap shoes make your own by taping metal bottle tops or ring-pulls to the soles of your shoes.

609 Perform an opera, but make the boys take on the shrieking soprano parts and the girls bellow out the low baritones.

610 **Stage a Viking invasion of your home. Loot, pillage and sing bawdy Nordic songs.**

SILLY SCORE

611 Have a steamy clinch with yourself. Go into the corner of a room, face the wall, and wrap your arms round your body so that your fingers are visible at the sides of your back. Now move your head in a passionate smooch and run your fingers up and down your sides. **Top marks for tastelessness!**

612 Got no audience? So what! Practise a comedy routine in front of a mirror, laughing at all your own jokes. See how long and loud you can giggle at each gag, then tickle yourself with a whole new style of titters and guffaws.

613 Pull-off a spoon somersault. Lay two large spoons on the table in front of you in a line, with the bowl of the first nearest you and the bowl of the second spoon slightly overlapping the end of the first. Now place your glass behind the end of the second spoon. When you whack your fist down on the bowl of the first spoon its end should flip up, flicking the bowl of the second spoon and causing it to somersault backwards and land in the glass. Impressive!

614 **Turn into a chinnykin!**
Draw a pair of eyes on your chin and a nose between the drawn-on eyes and your actual mouth. Tie a headscarf over your own eyes and nose then lie upside down on a sofa with your head hanging down backwards off the edge.

615 Have a laugh disguising yourselves as scary zombies. Root through the dressing-up box and slap on the face paints. Now thrill your family by performing 'Thriller'.

617 Try your hand at ice dancing without the skates... or the ice! You'll need a suitable partner and enough space to perfect your spinning axels and triple Salchows.

616 Tune the family radio to a classical music channel, then hide it out of sight. Take a seat at the dining room then perform a pretend piano concerto.

618 Make up some alternative words to 'Do-Re-Mi' from the Sound of Music. Here's a couple of lines to get you started: 'Mum, a lady with a great big bum, Dad an old git who is sad...'

619 Cheer up your bored best buddy by inviting him to experience life as a giant! Ask him to climb on your shoulders and pull on your dad's long mac. Button the coat up around you both and take the giant for a walk!

620 Make a human pyramid - you'll need at least six plucky people to pull it off! The first three should kneel on all fours on the ground, the next two should climb onto their backs then one final person can perch at the very top - arms in the air!

PUTTING ON A SHOW

135

621 Pick a famous drummer. Maybe you're inspired by your fave band or Animal from the Muppets? Get ready to play a mental drum solo using a pair of pencils. You've only rocked out if you've broken at least one of your 'sticks'.

ANiMAL CAPERS

622

Make your own pantomime horse!

Use your baby sister's hobby horse or draw a horse head on card and tape it to a broom handle. Climb on your 'steed', then cover yourself and a mate with a sheet. Gallop round the house or cavort like a bucking bronco.

624 Persuade three friends to join your barbershop quartet. Give each person one noise to perform – a tongue click, a squeak, a raspberry, or a yelp. Count yourselves in, then perform a marvellous medley. It may not be very tuneful, but your sound will definitely be unique!

623 **Pillow people**
Use fabric pens to draw a funny face onto an old pillowcase. Now put an anorak around your waist and zip it up tight so it hangs like a regular coat, but low enough for only your legs to be visible from the knee down. Ask a friend to put the pillow case over your head and then tuck it into the top of the coat. You've now transformed into a pillow person!

625 Put on a fist play. Tuck your thumb into your palm then view your hand from the side - it'll look like a gummy old man's mouth. Draw eyes on the side of your knuckle and move your thumb about to make the mouth move.

626 Pretend to run down a flight of stairs by bending your knees more ever so slightly with each forward step. You'll appear to be going downstairs even though you're on flat ground! This looks even funnier when your body is hidden from view behind a sofa.

136

627 Set up a pitch at the corner of your street and then transform yourself into a mime artist. White your face, rouge your cheeks and put black eyeliner crosses over your eyes. Act out a scene without speaking a word. Pretend you're standing behind an invisible glass wall or freeze like a statue, only moving to shout BOO into a spectator's ear!

628 Rouse your friends and neighbours with a garden performance of Swan Lake. Wet your faces and dip them in flour, dress up white undies or long johns then prance balletically all over the lawn. If you can find a couple of feathers to tape on your arms, even better!

ONE-MINUTE MADNESS

Have you got the X factor? Road test these silly suggestions to find out!

629 Standing in line for an ice cream? Treat everyone to a powerful Italian opera - Pavarotti style.

630 To earn extra showbiz points, perfect your stage-school grin and jazz hands. Just splay your fingers and waggle your palms.

631 Do the monkey walk. Stand in a row with at least three pals and link arms. Now walk forward crossing the right leg over the person on your right's left leg, and your left leg over the person on your left's right leg.

632 Grab a comb and wrap it with paper - put your mouth to it and squeak out a tune.

633 Get everyone to sit down ready for a show. Now run in and shout 'thank you very much, you've been a great audience, goodnight!'.

137

634 Next time the bell goes at the end of PE, shock your classmates with your rapidly beating heart. Pull your school sweater over your head, but stretch your arms out in front of you and thread your right hand into the left cuff. Withdraw your left arm from the sleeve and use it to make your heart pulse visibly underneath your jumper!

635 Turn yourself into a showbiz luvvie. Call everybody 'darling' and wear OTT glitzy outfits around the house. Offer to sign autographs, then present your mum with an outrageous list of demands.

WARNING: WACKY WIND-UP!

636 Make a show of biting off and swallowing one of your fingers, put it in your mouth, grit your teeth and shake your head from side to side as if your jaws are tearing at the flesh. With one big grunt rip your head away then reveal your remaining half finger (which is really folded towards your palm at the knuckle).

A SHOCKER FOR LITTLE KIDS!

637 For an instant crack-up, pretend to knock yourself out on a door frame. As you walk into a room, misjudge the opening and act out whacking your head. At the same time, kick your foot as hard as you can against the skirting board to make a wincingly loud cracking sound. Now fall on the floor as if you've been knocked out.

638 **Can you can can?** Rifle through your mum's wardrobe for her frilliest skirt and underpants. Get dressed up then high kick your way around the house. **Oh la la!**

639 **Are your folks hooked on TV medical dramas?**

Get some mates over, pull on white coats then recreate a hospital soap at home. Make it as dramatic as possible, squeezing tomato ketchup onto every casualty you deal with. Don't forget to regularly utter the lines:

'I think we're going to lose him...'

640 **Make up and learn a rap all about your freaky family!**

642 **Stand on your head and drink a glass of water – it may take several practise sessions before you can do this without getting soaked!**

641 Organize your buddies into a body orchestra. Gather in a semi-circle then make sounds out of yourselves! Use your hands to tap your knees, arms, chest, belly and head. For extra percussion pop your thumb out of your cheek and release bursts of piggy snorts.

643 **Ever fancied being a majorette?** Make a baton out of the long tube that comes inside a roll of gift-wrap, then paint it in a girly colour. When it's dry you're ready to have a whirl at twirling! Try flinging the baton into the air and catching it again whilst doing high kicks around the garden.

644 **Use a soft toy or a doll to put on a ventriloquist's show. Practise talking with your mouth closed and moving the toy as you make it speak.**

645 Become a contemporary artist, setting up a great work of modern art in the most inconvenient place possible. If your mum or nan tells you to clear it up, shoot them a look of outrage and sweep out of the room!

PUTTING ON A SHOW

MUSICAL MADNESS

PUTTING ON A SHOW

646 Put on a penguin chorus! Recruit your friends, then pull yellow rubber washing up gloves onto your feet. Waddle around, squawking in beautiful harmony.

647 Raid your little sis's wardrobe for a girlie dress, socks and shoes. Paint two red circles on your cheeks and dot some freckles on your nose. Now stand pigeon-toed and serenade your oldies with sickly-sweet show tunes. Just wait, your parents will soon be begging you to return to your usual, mischievous self!

648 Lace up your pretend inline skates and whirl round the kitchen tiles in your own interpretation of Starlight Express.

649 Act out the munchkin scenes from the Wizard of Oz, casting yourself and your mates as the little people. Crouch down, pull your T-shirts over your knees, then follow the yellow brick road.

140

WARNING: WACKY WIND-UP!

650 **When your mum calls you down for a particularly horrid dinner smudge your face with dirt or black make-up, grab a bowl and trudge into the kitchen singing** 'is it worth the waiting for, if we live til 84, all we ever get is gru-elll!!!' **from Oliver Twist.**

651 Perform 'A Whole New World' from the Little Mermaid with both legs squeezed into one, tail-like pyjama leg! ♪

652 Recreate the Jungle Book with your pets! Cast Buster the dog as Baloo and Tiddles the cat as Shere Khan. Now dance around them bawling out a gleeful version of the 'Bear Necessities'. You may find they can't stand the noise and flee!

Go singin' in the rain

653 Get dressed up in a raincoat and a hat, then open up your umbrella. Enlist your brother to shower you with water from a spray-bottle and you're ready to relive another magical musical moment!

654 **Baby brother and sister whingeing in your ear? Treat them to a scene they won't forget by taking on the part of the Child Catcher from Chitty Chitty Bang Bang. Offer the tots lollypops in a scarily sickly voice, then herd them into a cupboard at the last minute.**

PUTTING ON A SHOW

655 Make the most of your digital camera by scripting and filming an original home movie! Think of a plot, persuade your mates to be the actors then get shooting! Keep the bloopers on the memory stick for sniggering at later.

656 Tickle yourself by taking up beer mat flipping. Place a cardboard coaster on a table so that almost half of it is protruding past the table edge. Put your hand beneath the mat and with an upwards jerk flip the beer mat up and over, catching it on its way back down. Now try it with two or more coasters, it's actually easier with extra mats, but looks impressive!

657 You're a poet, did you know it? Write a funny verse or limerick, breaking it into short phrases. Write each line on a separate sheet of card in big letters. Get the cards in order, put on some jaunty music then reveal the poem by dropping each card from the stack. Your audience will howl as each funny line is revealed!

No great shakes

658 Working on a double act with a friend? Begin your routine with the great ankle shake! Approach each other with arms outstretched as if to shake hands, reach forward but miss and pass by each other. At the same time bring your outside foot off the floor, grab each other's ankles and shake vigorously.

659 Can you play the phone? Find a mobile or cordless handset, put it on loudspeaker, then punch in numbers so the tones make a tune.

660 Time to tune into *you tv*. If you're fed up with reruns, create some alternative programming starring... You. Get a cardboard box, cut a panel out of one side, draw buttons down the edge and place it over your head. Now read the news or become a chat show host!

QUICK & CRAZY

Short on time? No window of opportunity is too small to get wacky!! Here's a catalogue of **crazy stunts** you can pull in the blink of an eye. Each one of these **boredom busters** can be enjoyed right here, right now without a moment's thought about doing something more productive instead...

143

661 Say your sentences in reverse.

Reverse in sentences your say!

662 Next time you visit a busy burger bar, pretend to be suffering the effects of food poisoning.

WARNING: WACKY WIND-UP!

663 **Say 'WHY' to absolutely everything.**

664 **Pretend to be playing the most amazing video game... with the screen turned off.**

665 When your mum drags you to the cash machine, have a serious conversation with the ATM.

666 **Play imaginary golf in a public library.**

667 When it's raining, open your window and cry 'it's a beautiful day for ducks!'

668 See how long you can go without saying any words with the letter 'a' in them.

669 Try not to think about penguins.
This is trickier that you'd think - now that you've got the little critters in your head, it's almost impossible to herd them back out again!

670 Talk nonsense and cough loudly during your sister's favourite TV show.

671 Go green! Take a bath with without any water.

672 Talk about cheese all day to your friends.

674 When you're at home, put your hand up every time you want to ask someone a question.

675 Try to sing the alphabet, backwards.

673 Brain strain
Sit on a park bench then focus your attention on a random passer-by. Press hard on both temples, trying to use your mind power to command the stranger to do a specific action. Can you will them to turn left or look at their watch? Sooner or later one of your mind commands will come true, just wait and see!

QUICK & CRAZY

145

PARENT ALERT!

676 Next time your mum gives you a talking to, mirror her body movements exactly. When she picks up on it, avoid being grounded by insisting that you haven't got a clue what she is talking about!

677 See how many teaspoons you can hold in your mouth at the same time.

678 Refuse to use cutlery for a whole week. Can you survive off finger food or will Mum allow you to slurp up your spag bol?

680 Support a made-up football team for an entire season, inventing a whole new squad of players. Who's ready to take on Smirkchester United?

679 Eat something disgusting whilst riding your BMX!

681 Balance a piece of chocolate on your head and see how long it takes for someone to ask what on earth you are doing.

682 See how long you can hold a hum in class – inhale deeply and try and make the noise for a long as you can. Earn extra points for making your mates titter.

QUICK & CRAZY

683 Pick a random word or phrase out of a newspaper and repeat it over and over again until it becomes a meaningless set of noises.

684 Pinch yourself repeatedly to see if you can overcome your own pain threshold.

Ouch!

685 Scratch yourself, even if nothing itches. It feels amazing, doesn't it?

686 ## The ugly finder

Next time that your mum and dad have a posh party, burst into the room waving a broom. Shake the broom wildly in the direction of the guests. When asked what it is reply, 'it's an ugly finder and guess what, it's definitely working!!'

687 Head to the shopping mall with your best pal. Stand somewhere central then critique passing shoppers as harshly as you fancy! Give them marks out of ten for clothing, hairstyle and good looks; awarding bonus points for funny walks and crazy kids in tow.

GROSS OUT

688 Run outside in your granny's knickers!

689 **Invent a strange twitch like a head jerk or repeated blinking. See how long you can keep it up before your mum starts trying to take you to the doctor.**

690 Stand by a sliding door in a supermarket and make

sssCHWOOOOSH

noises every time it opens or shuts.

691 See if you can swallow your own tongue – a really stupid idea and pretty much impossible!

692 **Step off a kerb with your eyes closed and pretend it's a cliff.**

693 When you're next at the library, clamp your lips shut, look seriously at your book and make a low, annoying buzzing noise.

WEIRD OR WHAT?

694 Press your forehead against a mirror then stare hard into your eyes until you turn into a Cyclops.

695 Try and sound Welsh! You'll need to make sure your voice goes up at the end of your sentences so that everything sounds like a question. Add 'isn't it?' for extra realism. Once you've cracked that one, see what other accents you can pick up.

696 **Have a 'who is the least competitive?' competition. Trying to win this one will make sure you lose.**

QUICK & CRAZY

DOUBLE DARE

697 Persuade a pal to help you rifle through your neighbour's rubbish to see if you can work out what kind of person they are...

698 Tell everyone you meet that you're going to change your name by deedpoll to either Jeremiah Higginbottom or Flordeperia Farquaharson.

699 Make up a phrase that's never been said before.

700 Make yourself the monarch of your kingdom! Go round knighting family members whose behaviour pleases you and shun those whose conduct isn't servile enough.

701 Do a headstand then see if you can read a magazine upside-down.

QUICK & CRAZY

149

ONE-MINUTE MADNESS

These ideas are so speedy they're officially quicker than quick!

702 Try to screen kiss your family! Who squirms the most?

703 Say good morning every time you go to bed.

704 Look at the back of someone's head until they turn round - how long does it take them to sense your piercing stare?

705 Say the opposite of what you mean all day.

706 Jump up and down until you get a head-rush.

707 Pretend you're a monkey then pick fleas out of your mate's hair.

708 Parents on their only night out in months? Grin at the babysitter then howl like a dog at the door when they leave.

709 Work out your name backwards and adopt it from now on. If you're Tom Granger, you'll turn into Regnarg Mot.

710 Once you've sussed out your back-to-front name, practise your new reverse signature.

QUICK & CRAZY

711 Try to punch a hole in a piece of paper using just your tongue. If you can't do it you better start working out that muscle with some tongue press-ups.

712 LOL TXT chat
Confuse your granny or someone from an older generation by sending them a text message using only short abbreviations.

713 Make up the craziest excuse ever for not having done your homework. How about 'my Aunt Jenny's pet platypus relieved itself on my notebook, Sir!'

714 Have a go at drawing a life-size giraffe!

715 Pretend all humans are about to perish from a strange disease, apart from the people standing in your sitting room...

MUSCLE BOY!

716 Put nude tights on your arms and fill them with hankies to make incredible biceps.

QUICK & CRAZY

151

TICK TOCK IT'S WACKY O'CLOCK!

717 Rope in some friends to make a group of 14 people. Lie down on the grass and create a living clock face! There should be a person for each of the numbers and two human 'hands'.

718 Synchronize watches with a friend and try to do the same things at the same times of the day. Phone each other on the hour to check you're still on track.

719 **Wacky races**
Time each other running backwards round your school field. Add in a three-legged sprint and piggyback hurdles, too!

720 Try wearing your watch on your ankle for the day. Whenever you need to check the time grab onto your foot.

721 Try using the sun instead of a watch for a week. If you're late for class or for your tea tell the grown-up that you're uncommonly interested in Scandinavian Daymarks! Daymarks are a way of telling the time without a clock, but not many people know that.

YOU MUST BE JOKING!

722 See how many watches you can wear on your arm at once - make sure that they're visible over your clothes! Now go out into town and ask people if they have the time.

723 Make your own old-fashioned pocket watch. Find an old stopwatch and suspend it on a necklace chain. Tuck it into the breast pocket of your shirt or jacket then consult it seriously every now and then.

724 Pretend to be the White Rabbit from Alice in Wonderland! Fuss round the house chivvying everyone along and telling them you're all going to be very late. Just don't explain what for...

725 Wear a watch that's completely at odds with your style! Borrow your kid sister's pink princess model or try a clunky one that's actually made of wood. If you're a girl, go large and sport your dad's massive manly timepiece for the day.

QUICK & CRAZY

153

ANIMAL CAPERS

726 Provide the commentary for an imaginary football game between your goldfish.

727 Pull the weirdest face you can.

728 Pretend to be severely allergic to sunlight, cats, dus and green vegetable

730 Lie on your back on the floor. Now see if you can get your feet up by your ears.

729 Put your parents' favourite sayings to the test. Pull a face and hold it to see if the wind will actually change and keep you that way. Gorge on too much chocolate to find out if you'll really turn into a bar. Don't eat your crusts then see if you start getting unhealthy. If the sayings turn out to be rubbish, confront your oldies with their bare-faced lies and demand recompense.

731 Drink a glass of milk then jump up and down like a loony – if anyone asks, say you're making a DIY milkshake.

732 Try to talk just like your mum for an hour.

QUICK & CRAZY

733 Pretend you're James Bond!! Refer to your mum as 'Ms Moneypenny', your dad as 'M' and tell them that you'd like your juice 'shaken, not stirred'.

734 See an image through your eyelids. Stare at a picture for a minute, then shut your eyes - you'll find that you can see the 'after image' for about the same time again. It helps if you push gently on your eyelids, too.

735 Burp in time to the theme tune of your mum's favourite soap.

736 Fall truly, madly, deeply in love with an inanimate household object and refuse to be parted from it.

QUICK & CRAZY

737 Become a beetle
Lie on your back with your legs waving in the air until someone helps you get upright.

738 Make your own Mr Potato Head using coloured drawing pins and a spud.

SILLY SCORE

740 Try to crack the world record in something daft like not blinking. You'll probably struggle to do a minute but the world record is over 30 hours! Too tough? Give finger snapping a bash. Can you do 24 clicks on the same hand in under 5 seconds?

TOP PRANK

739 Tell your parents that you've booked a family holiday to the Maldives on their credit card. Make sure you do your homework so that you can quote the right resort, flight times, dates and the astronomical price tag.

741 Get down on all fours to see the world from the unique point of view of your pet! Meow or bark a little for atmosphere.

742 Swap your bother and your dad's underwear drawers around and see who notices first!

HOLIDAY HILARITY

Schools out forever! OK, maybe not forever, but for a few weeks at least. When the holidays come round you've got days on end to devote to **insane** time-wasting and **bonkers** behaviour. The **seasonal sillies** in this section will drive your parents **mental**, whilst keeping you in stitches from Valentine's Day to New Year's Eve.

743 Dress up as the Easter Bunny on Christmas Day. You're guaranteed to make an entrance as you skip downstairs to open your pressies!

744 On the first day of the summer holidays, stun your mum by getting ready for school.

745 No chance of a white Christmas this year? Never mind, head outside and make a brown snowman out of sludgy mud instead!

746 Send adoring Valentine's cards to your teacher signed by your class mates. Choose slushy hearts and cupids, make up lurve poems and cover the envelopes with masses of kisses.

747 Put a small marble into a box, then place that into a bigger one. Keep layering up with larger and larger boxes until the final package is as massive as you can get. Now wrap the whole thing in a layer of gift-wrap and hand it to your older sister. Her eyes will light up when she thinks that you've shelled out a fortune on a huge Christmas pressie.

WARNING: WACKY WIND-UP!

748 **Run over to the pool of your holiday complex and shout 'SHARK!!!'**

749 Next time you have a day trip to the beach, put on your sister's bikini! Wander down to the water as if nothing's amiss.

750 **No chance of a skiing trip this winter hols? Pretend to ski down a very busy street instead, sliding your legs forward and back. Make poles out of garden canes, then wave jauntily to the people that you pass.**

751 A long car journey to your holiday destination is the ideal time to make up some nutty backseat rituals. Tell your passengers to hold their breaths whenever you pass a graveyard and salute every time you spot a yellow car.

752 **Pass the time on the plane journey to your holiday hotspot by pretending to drop off on the shoulder of the passenger next to you. Flop across them, drool heavily then start snoring!**

HOLIDAY HILARITY

159

753 Make the most of St Patrick's Day by shouting 'top o' the morning to ya!' at every bewildered person that you pass on the way to school.

754 **Rain ruining your holiday?** Don't cower inside, have a pool party anyway! Grab your cossie and enjoy the extra showers.

755 On Easter Day present the family with a painted box of eggs. Wait for their faces to fall when they realise that you've bought real eggs rather than the yummy chocolate variety.

756 **Go Christmas carolling in June - a warbled rendition of Ding Dong Merrily On High is soooo much funnier in 90° heat! If you're on holiday in Oz go traditional and do things the other way round.**

HOLIDAY HILARITY

757 Try to make the cringiest family Christmas photo you can. Get everyone to wear dreadful snowflake-covered jumpers, Santa hats and novelty festive earrings. It you manage to pull it off, you could even use it as your comedy Xmas card next year!

758 During the holiday packing empty your sister's case and carefully fill it with your own stuff. If you're feeling really mean, you could also replace her summer swimsuit with a pair of earmuffs and gloves.

759 Just before you go away on holiday, nip into the car and change your dad's sat nav voice instructions into Croatian.

760 Smudged shades

Rub butter or margarine all over your hands, then offer to clean your parents' sunglasses. They'll be squinting through the smears all afternoon.

ANIMAL CAPERS

761 Chinese New Year is the ideal time to find out about your birth animal. Were you born in the year of the Tiger, Dragon or Snake? Look your creature up on the net then behave like one all day. Monkey-born kids should be seen scoffing bananas and swinging off the furniture while junior rats should steal food whenever they can.

HOLIDAY HILARITY

ONE-MINUTE MADNESS

Up for fun in the sun? These holiday wheezes are super-silly and super-snappy!

763 Head down to the beach wearing a pair of flippers and your baby brother's rubber ring.

764 On a ferry or boat? Sit on deck and row with imaginary oars.

765 Create a crazy sand creature, like a Loch Ness Monster with humps. Press on shells, scales and seaweed fins.

766 Ring room service and order a 4 am wake-up call for your parents.

767 Swim a length of your pool doing the most pathetic, splashy doggy paddle you can muster.

762 When you're away camping, wait till everyone's asleep then sneak outside and make scary wild animal noises.

768 The night before you go off on your annual break, tell your parents that someone from the airline called to say there's been a problem with the booking.

Yucky Yule
769 Pick some sprigs of mistletoe then make unlikely couples pucker up by holding it over them. How about your teen sister and mad old grandpa Norman? Or maybe your dad with pushy Mrs Miggins from next door?

770 Document your alternative Christmas! We all know that in real-life the turkey will be overdone, your granny will fall asleep in front of the TV, and your cousins will end up rowing over their new computer game. Capture these precious moments on camera then stick them lovingly into a scrapbook.

772 No flash holidays this time around? Pretend to jet off somewhere exotic and devise your own no-expense-spared holiday itinerary. Pack, find some nice accommodation (maybe your parents' room), then go on an adventure around town, safari trek the park and scuba-dive at the local pool.

771 Make a silly cheque book out of an old notepad, designing blank cheques that you can fill in and give out to your mates instead of birthday presents. Each cheque should be made out with a daft pledge that will make them chuckle. Why not promise to put a whoopee cushion on your teacher's chair?

773 Just before you go away for the summer, swap your dad's board shorts for that ancient pair of tight budgie-smuggler trunks nestling in the bottom of his drawer.

YOU MUST BE JOKING!

774 Declare your own national holiday! Perhaps the world needs a Mole Appreciation Day or time out to consider Free Ice-cream For All. Circle the date in your diary, spread the word and look horrified if your mum even suggests going to school.

775 Going to France this year? Confuse things by swotting up on German or Spanish vocab then put your new knowledge to the test in the local shops and restaurants.

776 This Christmas use your pocket money to buy cotton wool balls then see if you can create a winter wonderland on your bedroom window sill!

777 Liven up your summer hols by digging a small hole in the sand and half burying your shoes so that the toes are sticking out. Now move back about three metres and dig a shallow ditch to lie in. Get someone to cover you with sand so that just your head and shoulders are sticking out. Now it looks as if you're the world's tallest child!

778 Why not surprise your parents on Valentine's Day with a heart-shaped box of chocolates? Before you hand over the goodies, snaffle the chocs and tape the lid shut using double-sided tape inside the lid – watching your dad trying to open the box will be a complete scream!

779 Pretend to ice-dance in your holiday swimming pool. Swirl about for a moment, then suddenly look up in realisation and shout 'Help! **The ice has melted!!!'**

780 On your next summer holiday wait till your big sis goes for a swim, then move all her stuff! Switch her towel from the perfectly-placed sun lounger in full sunshine to the broken deckchair hidden in the shade next to the bins.

781 Next time you're on a plane, tell the air hostess that you're a fruitarian. Explain that you can only eat fruit that falls naturally from trees and insist that she adjusts your flight meal accordingly.

782 Travelling to foreign climes? Pretend to be a local, giving out directions to hapless tourists in heavily accented English.

HOLIDAY HILARITY

HAUNTED HI-JINX

783 Crack 'em up with this creepy joke:

Q: What's a ghost's favourite fairytale?
A: Ghouldilocks and the Three Bears.

784 Make a headless costume out of an over-sized skirt or trousers. Fold a large piece of cardboard into a tube that will fit on top of your head and cover the top of the tube with a piece of red material to create a bloody severed neck. Now place the tube on your head and pull on an adult's shirt sticking the collar to the bottom of the tube. Stick your head through the front of the shirt and get a friend to do up the buttons above and below your face. Pull on a skirt or trousers up to your armpits and tuck the shirt in. Pin the arms of the shirt under your chin so it looks like you're holding your own head.

Gruesome!

785 **Halloween's the time for freaking out your folks. Set your alarm for the dead of midnight then do your loudest scream ever.**

786 **Invite your gang for a Halloween sleepover, then put on a scary movie. Turn off all the lights and hand round the cushions!**

166

787 Spook your friends out with the best ghost story ever! Tell the tale of a young lad that died in mysterious circumstances on Halloween. Now dim the lights, then pass around a bag asking people to 'feel' the evidence for themselves. First hand round his fingers (wet, peeled carrots), then dare your mates to touch his eyes (two tinned lychees), shattered teeth come next (individual sweetcorn) and lastly his brain (sticky spaghetti). By the end your pals will be quivering wrecks!

788 ## The puking pumpkin

When your dad carves the face on your pumpkin, get him to keep the sick-looking centre full of pips. Feed the seeds out through the mouth to make it look like your Jack O'Lantern just threw up.

789 Make a severed finger! Get a small empty box and cut a finger-sized hole in the bottom. Arrange some cotton wool along the base of the box. Holding the carton flat on your palm poke your middle finger up through the hole and lay it on the cotton wool. Decorate the end with ketchup to make it look as if it's been cut off. Put the lid on and offer the box to a friend.

HOLIDAY HILARITY

790 When you're away in Costa del Crazy, freak people out by swimming under their legs while they're minding their own business in the pool.

791 Start a game of Li-lo Polo! All you need is a pair of inflatable sunbeds and a ball. The idea is to get the ball to the opposite end of the pool and past your opponent without splashing off your sunbed.

792 **Try sand sledging** Find some dunes, grab a couple of inflatable lilos and get racing.

793 While away a long car journey with the most annoying, repetitive song you can think of. Work your way through '1,000 green bottles, hanging on the wall', seeing how far you get before your folks pull over and give you a right rollicking.

GROSS OUT

794 Create an Easter egg with a difference! Use a big needle to poke a hole in the shell of an egg. Now wrap the egg in foil and leave it in the sunshine to ferment for a few hours. When you're ready to have some fun, go into the garden and drop the egg on the patio. The air will fill with the most putrid smell ever!

795 Try to eat a different flavour ice cream every day of your holiday.

796 Give your family holiday names suited to your destination and use them the whole time. Try out Juan, Carlos and Carmelita, or go for Hans, Ernst and Brunhilda.

798 People do silly things when the sun's out! Prove it on holiday by persuading your dad that he'd look really 'young and cool' if he got his hair braided or had a tattoo from a street stall.

799 On the first day that you arrive at your holiday resort, do the biggest belly flop in the pool that you can muster.

800 Tacky tourist
Use your pocket money to buy the most outlandish holiday get-up you can find. Think grass skirts, garlands and coconuts, or sombreros and loud ponchos. Now wear it every day till you go back to school.

797 Wear your cosiest hat, scarf, gloves and coat on the hottest day of the year.

HOLIDAY HILARITY

801 Holidaying in a camping park this year? Play Knock Down Ginger on all the caravan doors.

802 Brighten up New Year's Eve by writing a list of ridiculous resolutions. Promise to only hop on a Tuesday, change your middle name to 'Danger' and start collecting cola cans.

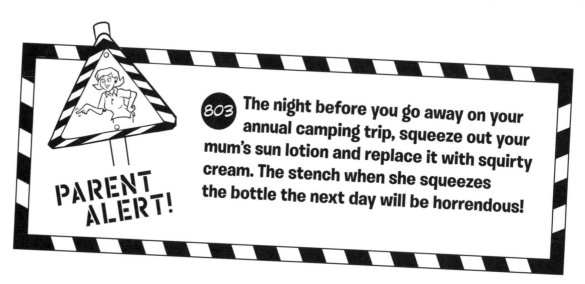

PARENT ALERT!

803 The night before you go away on your annual camping trip, squeeze out your mum's sun lotion and replace it with squirty cream. The stench when she squeezes the bottle the next day will be horrendous!

804 Get your little brother panicking by questioning his place on Santa's Christmas list! Grab a blank exercise book and write NAUGHTY in big letters on the first page, then flip it over and write NICE on the first page at the back. Using your best handwriting, fill both ends with a list of names. Make a point of burying your brother's name somewhere in the middle of the naughty list, then leave it lying around near the tree. Convince him that one of the elves must have dropped it!

KITCHEN CAPERS

Watch out, Mum, the kids are **invading the kitchen!** There are so many silly and downright daft things that you can do with **food**. Grab a tea towel and tie it round your head, then **steam** into the **Cooking Zone!** This chapter is crammed with ideas for **kitchen commandos** so get **cracking** and see how much trouble you can **stir up** before it's time for tea?

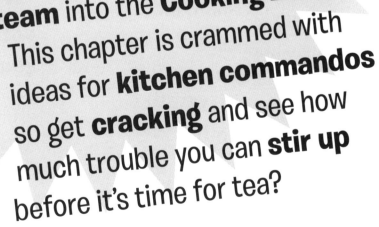

MIGHTY MESSY

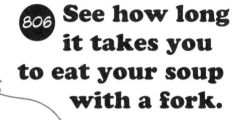

806 See how long it takes you to eat your soup with a fork.

805 Have a friend stand behind you, close his eyes and poke his arms through yours. Now talk him through the steps of a recipe and see if can pull off each stage without missing the bowl or dropping the spoon! Stick to something simple and don't try anything that needs cutting or dicing.

807 Take the labels off the canned food and watch the cook overheat! (Don't tell them you've written the contents on the bottom of each can!)

808 Find out how high you can throw an egg without it breaking when you catch it.

809 Persuade your mum to make pancakes! Get two frying pans and have a flipping competition with your sister or brother. Once you've got the hang of it, try flinging between the pans, too. All dropped pancakes go to the dog.

810 See who can suck on a boiled sweet longest without crunching.

811 Mashosaurus

Make a mashed potato dinosaur by scooping creamed spuds onto the plate in the shape of a head, long neck and body. Now squish on carrot batons for legs, asparagus tips for the spines on its back and tail, half an olive for an eye and tiny pepper triangles for teeth. Eat it before it eats you!

812 Paint a picture using brown sauce, mustard and creamy mayo.

813 Treat your parents to breakfast in bed. Tempt them with a delicious menu, then load up their trays with plastic toy food.

814 Blindfold the family and read out the ingredients on the back of packets of food and cans of fruit and veg. Who can guess what the food is? The loser has to create a special meal using all the foods they didn't guess. Might be time to visit your nan for tea!

KITCHEN CAPERS

YOU MUST BE **JOKING!**

815 Play egg roulette! Hard boil enough eggs so that you have one per player, but when they're cooled replace one cooked egg with a raw one. Now put all the eggs in a bowl and ask your pals to pick one each. You can choose to switch with someone else as long as they agree. On the count of three all smash your eggs against your forehead! One person will be in for a yucky surprise.

816 ## Mum badgering you to eat healthily?

Do it your way with this creative candle salad. You'll need a banana, a pineapple ring, some lettuce leaves, some slivers of raw carrot and a cocktail stick. Cut the banana in half crossways and stand it up on the cut end in the middle of the pineapple ring which in turn has been placed on lettuce leaves. Trim the pointed end off the banana, then cut a flame-shaped sliver of carrot and attach it to the top of the banana with the cocktail stick.

817 Help serve the dishes at your next family meal, whilst pretending to be an outspoken celebrity chef.

818 Try eating with your knife and fork switched the wrong way round.

819 Try and make your breakfast to music. Enlist your sis or bro, put a cool tune on the radio then see if you can pop and pass your toast, spread the marmalade and pour the juice in time to the beat.

820 **Next time your mum makes a boring salad for lunch, liven it up with some natural inhabitants! Either pick fake bugs and secrete them among the lettuce leaves or for a total freak-out collect some real ones! You'll be having a take-away before you know it.**

821 Run an experiment to see how many pieces of popcorn you can put in your mouth at one time.

822 **Wear a milk moustache for as long as you can without wiping it off on your cuff.**

823 **See how many marshmallows you can munch through in five minutes.**

824 Try drinking water from the other side of a glass.

WARNING: WACKY WIND-UP!

825 Scrape the jam out of a doughnut and replace it with ketchup. Push the dough back in place then give it to someone who has been getting on your nerves recently.

KITCHEN CAPERS

826 Bake a completely new dish, devising your own ingredients list and recipe steps! Before sharing out your new signature dish, road test the meal on your dad.

827 We've all managed second helpings of a meal from time to time, but what about thirds or fourths? See how many helpings you can swallow in one sitting. If your mum looks worried tell her that you have a tape worm.

828 How many peas can you balance on your fork at one time without the aid of a condiment like ketchup, brown sauce or mayo?

829 Make a crazy super-stacked sandwich using all your favourite fillings at once. If peanut butter goes with jam, what new crazy combinations can you discover?

TOP PRANK

830 Dip Brussels sprouts in melted chocolate, allow them to dry then give them to people as sweet treats!

831 Do the crisp challenge! Blindfold your best mate then give him six flavours of crisps to munch on. Can he tell his salt 'n' vinegar from his prawn cocktail?

KITCHEN CAPERS

176

832 Have a game of frisbee with a pile of ring doughnuts. Catch the spinning dough disk in your hand or your mouth!

833 Cut letters out of potatoes and make some potato print ransom notes. How about 'HEY SIS, DO MY CHORES THIS WEEK OR DOLLY GETS IT'?

834 Rustle up some fart food! Make the windiest meal you can using whiffy foods like baked beans, Brussels sprouts, hummus and eggs.

GROSS OUT

835 Ever wonder how your meal would look inside your tummy? Scoop everything on your plate into a blender, then give it a whirl. Now pour the gloop into a glass and drink! **Yum!**

KITCHEN CAPERS

177

836 Cracker stacks

Create a towering lunch using crackers and various fillings such as slices of ham, salami, cheese or tomatoes. Alternate a slice of each with a cracker and see how high you can build your snack-scraper.

837 Scoff on ice-cream till you get brain freeze!

838 Make some lovely fairy cakes, then whisk in some crazy yellow or blue food colouring. Use writing icing and decorations to turn them into a batch of mini-monster cakes.

839 Choco-mazing!

Melt some chocolate and line a baking tin with greaseproof paper. Use a spoon to splat the soft brown mixture across the paper to make a large, web-like maze. Stick a sweet in the centre, then wait for it to dry. When the chocolate hardens, peel the maze off and munch your way to the middle.

840

You've heard of **Banana Man**? The world needs another food-related superhero! **Broccoli Boy** perhaps? Or the **Incredible Cheese Girl**? To get started, lay an edible item on a sheet of paper then draw on legs, arms, weapons and a cape.

KITCHEN CAPERS

ONE-MINUTE MADNESS

Every meal's a happy meal when you add a little wackiness! Check out these crazy cook's tips.

841 Keep a straw in your pocket and use it to noisily slurp up all your drinks.

842 See how many gherkins you and your best mate can eat. Bet you won't get far before you both are begging to get down from the table!

843 Make a saucepan drum kit and rock out!

844 Chew everything 20 times before you swallow.

845 See if you can sit at one end of the kitchen counter and have your mum slide your cup of juice down to you from the other end, just like they did in the Wild West.

846 Try spoon tuning. Hold a pair of spoons back-to-back with your index finger between them to act as a pivot. Now bash the heads against the other hand or your thigh so that the bowls hit each other with a clack. Play a spoony metal tune.

847 Before sitting down to a family meal, turn the sauce bottles upside down so that the sauce sloshes out quicker than anyone thinks it's going to. When everyone takes their places sing 'shake and shake the ketchup bottle, none will come and then a lot'll!'

KITCHEN CAPERS

179

848 Tiptoe into the kitchen and empty out your salt cellar. Fill it up with granulated sugar, then pop it back into the cupboard.

849 Write cryptic notes saying things like 'at least this is a fortune message, it could have been a caterpillar' then sneak them into other people's sandwiches at lunchtime.

850 **Whip up a bug-tastic snack!** Put digestive biscuits or crackers into a ziplock sandwich bag, then pound it with a rolling pin until they're reduced to dust. Open the bag and drop in a few chocolate sprinkles. Now shake and chow down - it'll look like you're eating insect-ridden sand.

851 **Bend it like Beckham** Test your soccer skills using old fruit and veg instead of a football. How does it feel to take a penalty with an apple, a melon or a head of cauliflower. Can you pass, dribble and score a fruity hat-trick?

852 Peanut Butter Goo tastes yummy but looks as if someone has lost control of their bowels on your plate! Blend 200g of peanut butter, with 200g plain yoghurt, 100g of Rice Crispies and 2 tablespoons of dried coconut. Enjoy!

853 Stuff hankies, old socks or scarves down the front of your sis's dolls' clothes to make them look as if though they've just finished a huge meal!

854 **Have a blue day or green or orange. Add food colouring to all your meals for a day. Does the colour make the food taste better or worse?**

MIGHTY MESSY

855 Next time you have a friend to tea, play the blindfold food game! Sit next to the fridge and tie a scarf round your friend's eyes. Open the fridge door and start feeding your pal a variety of food, challenging them to guess what each mouthful might be. It's much harder to tell without the sense of sight.

856 Have a food fight! You'll get in a lot of trouble for this, but less if you clean up straight away afterwards. Cold pasta makes good ammo, as do old cold roast potatoes and any dessert featuring whipped cream or custard.

LET'S GET FRUITY

857 Make a crazy smoothie using all the fruit and vegetables you can lay yours hands on.

858 Tongue-tie a cherry stem. See if you can pop a cherry stem in your mouth and tie it in a knot using only your tongue and teeth. Apparently a few people can do it – are you one of them?

859 Place 22 grapes on the table in a football formation. Use white grapes for one team and purple grapes for the other. Choose a big grape to be the ball, then flick and squash your way to victory.

860 Have a go at fruit squirting! Get some old clothes on and load up with juicy fruit (yes, tomatoes count!). Now try to squirt your opponent into submission.

Grape escape

861 Prop a banana up against the side of your fruit bowl and place all the other fruit in a line on the table as if they've used the banana as an escape ladder and are making a bid for freedom!

862 Tape bunches of bananas to your wrists and see how much you can do with fruity fingers.

863 Put on your mum's biggest bra then fill it with apples, oranges or even melons.

864 Make your own Carmen Miranda hat! Find a hat with a wide brim then place the contents of your fruit bowl on top of it, using tape to hold any wobbly bits in place. Now you're ready to dance around exotically.

865 Arrange the contents of your fruit bowl into a shape or the figure of a man or a dog. Get out your sketchbook, and draw your own silly still life.

WEIRD OR WHAT?

866 Peel a large apple and brush it with lemon juice mixed with a teaspoon of salt. Carve out a mean face, using raisins and cloves for eyes and teeth, then put the apple somewhere warm for a couple of weeks. When it's dried out, the fruit will transform into a sinister, shrunken head!

KITCHEN CAPERS

PARENT ALERT!

867 Make your mum paranoid by secretly coming down in the middle of the night and arranging everything in her cupboards or fridge in alphabetical order. If you pull this off several nights running she'll be even more freaked out!

868 Return of the blob!
Ever heard of that old horror movie where strange gloop takes over the world and swallows everything in its path? Make your own spooky slime using two parts cornflour to one part water and add drops of red food colouring. Mix it until smooth and then blob out, sinking your fingers into the squidgy mess.

869 Alien fridge magnets
In a saucepan, mix 450g of baking soda with 150g cornflour. Gradually add 200g cups water and stir until smooth. Cook your mixture over a medium heat, until it's thick and dough-like. Knead the clay and flatten it out. Use a blunt knife to cut out loads of weird alien face shapes, then let them dry overnight. Stick on googly eyes and a small magnet at the back and your life forms are ready to explore the fridge!

870 If your mum says you're getting no other food until you finish your veg - test her mettle. How many times will she continue serving up your cold, unfinished meal before giving up? She'll probably crack within hours, long before you do.

BRILL BRAINBUSTERS

Just because you're a crazy cat who likes to fool around, that doesn't mean you don't have any grey stuff upstairs! This brill, boredom-bashing chapter is packed with loads of gigglesome ways to give your brain a really wacky workout.

Got brain strain?
Answers to the most torturous brain teasers are printed upside-down at the bottom of each page.

871 How good is the connection between your mouth and your brain? Test it out by saying this tongue twister three times in a row: 'any noise annoys an oyster, but a noisy noise annoys an oyster more.'

872 Give your tongue a workout with this silly twister! Say 'unique New York' over and over as quickly as you can.

873 Make a wacky word search for a friend! Draw a 10x10 grid on squared paper and fill it with loony words like 'mental', 'crazy' and 'zany'. Write these in a list at the bottom and fill the rest of the squares with random letters. Now see how long it takes your mate to complete it.

874 Calculate how old you would you be if you lived to the year 3004 AD.

875 What has two arms and a neck but no head?

SILLY SCORE

876 Time yourself saying the alphabet forwards, then see how fast you can say it backwards! Pit your wits against a pal, until you're able to get the backwards time quicker than the forwards one!

877 What phrase or word does this bonkers brainbuster represent?

J J J E
J J E J
J E J J
E J J J

Answers: **875:** A jumper. **877:** Diagonally.

878 Create your own secret code

Draw 26 symbols for the letters of the alphabet or create a number code where A=1, B=2, C=3 and so on. Keep your key in a special hiding place, then challenge your dad to decipher a cheeky coded message!

879 Ask your mum to put 15 different items on a tray, then cover them up with a tea-towel. Uncover the tray for a couple of minutes, study the objects and then hide them again. Take out a paper and pen and try to list everything you've seen. You have five minutes, starting... now!

880 See how many three and four letter words you can make out of your full name in five minutes. Include all your middle names and any silly nicknames that you're known by.

881 Imagine you were being followed by a rampaging bull. **How would you survive?**

BRILL BRAINBUSTERS

Answers: **881:** Stop imagining!

187

882 **Can you decipher the common phrase from this wacky word block?**

T M C D
A U O G
H S M P
W T E N

883 Grab a calculator and figure out your mates' ages by how often they eat chocolate. How many times a week do they eat chocolate - choose a number between 1 and 10. Multiply that by 2. Add 5. Multiply by 50. Add the current year (all four digits). If they've had a birthday this year take away 250. If not, take away 251. Subtract the year they were born. Hey presto, you'll end up with your friend's age and how many times they eat chocolate!

884 Read this sentence:

FINISHED FILES ARE THE RESULT OF YEARS OF SCIENTIFIC STUDY COMBINED WITH THE EXPERIENCE OF YEARS.

Now count how many Fs are in the sentence - check out your answer before counting again!

885 Stare out of your window for five minutes, looking out for interesting stuff outside. Now move away from the glass, grab a sketchpad and draw the scene you've just studied, but change the objects to wacky alternatives beginning with the same letter! So if you saw a bird, why not change it to Batman, or a car to a candle with wheels!

886 Give your brain a spring clean. Pick a wacky word that means absolutely nothing, like 'boozlyflip'. Now sit in a quiet room and chant your word over and over until your mind clears.

ONE-MINUTE MADNESS

Complete these sentences using the initial letters as a clue – how quickly can you guess the connection?

887 8 l on a s

888 60 s in a m

889 S W and the 7 D

890 10 t on 2 f

891 4 s to a s

892 8 l on an o

894 Work your body language to the limit! Lay down then try to spell out a funny phrase or shape while your folks spectate from the sofa.

893 Put on a blindfold then get a friend to play a tune on a keyboard, recorder or guitar using just three notes. Listen hard, then whip the blindfold off and try it play it back again from memory. Once you can play the tune by ear, try longer tunes using four, five and six notes.

BRILL BRAINBUSTERS

Answers: **One-minute madness: 887:** 8 legs on a spider. **888:** 60 seconds in a minute. **889:** Snow White and the Seven Dwarfs. **890:** 10 toes on 2 feet. **891:** 4 sides to a square. **892:** 8 legs on an octopus.

896 Look at this number sequence for as long as it takes you to think you've committed every character to your brain:

L7PJJ5213RUBBOI2

Now look away and write the sequence down. Did you get it spot on?

895 Do some dippy digging! Bury some tiny toys along the flowerbeds of your garden, covering them over with soil. Give it a day or two, then try and uncover them all first time.

897 What are tree mistake in this sentence?

WEiRD OR WHAT?

898 Check out this fascinating fact: aoocrdnig to rscheearch, it dseno't mtaetr in waht oerdr the ltteres in a wrod are, the olny iproamtnt tihng is taht the frsit and lsat ltteer be in the rghit pclae. Tihs is bcuseae the huamn mnid deos not raed ervey lteter by istlef, but the wrod as a wlohe.

Answers: **897:** (1) 'tree' should be spelt 'three' (2) 'mistake' should have an 's' on the end (3) there isn't a third mistake!

DOUBLE DARE

899 Make up a riddle about a boy or girl in your class that you like, then challenge your best mate to guess their identity.

900 Try saying **'red lorry, yellow lorry'** 20 times without making a single mistake.

901 Make up personalised number plates for your neighbours' cars using numbers and letters. Try to base them on their characters - so the smelly student next door could have **'GRO 55'**.

902 Try making up an 'alliterative sentence'. That's a posh way of making a phrase where every word starts with the same first letter!

904 I am sometimes strong, and sometimes weak, but I am nobody's fool. For there is no language that I cannot speak though I never went to school What am I?

903 Play this as a team or with a mate. Choose a subject, such as ice cream flavours. Someone has to say the alphabet in their head. Say 'stop' and whatever letter they are on you have to quickly think of 5 flavours beginning with that letter. The losers have to do a crazy forfeit.

905 **Potty pictures**
Draw a wacky class portrait by using the words in people's names to create a picture of them. For example, if there is someone called Sarah Melrose, draw Sarah eating melons in a rose garden!

BRILL BRAINBUSTERS

906 Say silk three times very quickly. Now spell it. Now say what it is that cows drink?

907 Try to write down every piece of clothing in your wardrobe. No peeking!

909 Sneak into your brother or sister's bedroom when they're not around. Now spend 10 minutes looking at the ornaments, frames and toys on their bookcase or dressing table. Try messing up everything and then putting it back exactly as it was before. Think hard - if you don't do it right, you'll be in big trouble!

908 Can you say this phrase without grinning or getting in a muddle? 'Which watch did which witch wear and which witch wore which watch?'

910 Love building stuff with Lego bricks? Challenge a friend to a tower building race – who can build the tallest tower before it topples?

Answers: **906**: Water - bet you said 'milk'!

ANIMAL CAPERS

911

See if you can work out how tall you'd be in hands - the unit of length that is used to measure horses. One horse hand is 10 centimetres. Are you the human equivalent of a grand old Shire or a tiny Shetland pony?

912 **Pool patterns**

Next time you go for a dip, give your brain and your body a watery workout! Create a new swim stroke - doggy paddle legs with butterfly movement arms? Watch and see if it catches on with the other swimmers at the pool.

913 If a plane crashes flying over a foreign country, would you bury the survivors in the place where the plane crashed or take them back to where they lived?

ONE-MINUTE MADNESS

Ready to baffle your brother and stun your sis with your amazing quick wits?

914 Try remembering everything you've eaten for breakfast, lunch and dinner for the last week.

915 Name as many different kinds of footwear as you can in 60 seconds. Extra points for inventing wacky new ones!

916 Give yourself one minute to write down all the words you know beginning with W. We'll give you 'wacky' to start you off!

917 Act out as many nursery rhymes as you can for a mate to guess in one minute.

918 Give your best friend 60 seconds to list your ten favourite things in the world - now do the same for them.

RIDDLE ME THIS!

919 There's a shipwreck and every single person is lost at sea, but two survive. How is this possible?

920 I have streets but no pavement, I have cities but no skyscrapers, I have lakes yet no water, I have woods but no trees. What am I?

922 A hole leading in, a hole leading out, I connect to a cavern that is slimy throughout. **What am I?**

921 How much dirt would there be in a round hole that is two metres deep and two metres wide?

923 You are in a house with four windows that all face south. A bear walks by - **what colour is it?**

BRILL BRAINBUSTERS

Answers: **919:** They were married. **920:** A map. **921:** None, it's a hole, silly! **922:** Your nose. **923:** White. It has to be a polar bear, as you could only be at the North Pole for all windows to face south.

924 If a red house is made from red bricks, and a white house is made from white bricks, what is a green house made from?

925 Which cheese is made backwards?

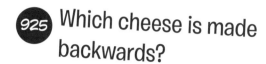

927 What do you put in a toaster?

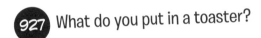

926 How do you make one disappear?

929 What's so fragile even saying its name can break it?

928 What seven letter word becomes longer when the third letter is removed?

930 A man and his son were in a car accident. The man died on the way to the hospital, but the boy was rushed into surgery. The surgeon said 'I can't operate, that's my son!' **How is this possible?**

931 Which is light as a feather, yet even the strongest man cannot hold it for more than a few minutes?

932 Which word, if pronounced right, is wrong, but if pronounced wrong is right?

BRILL BRAINBUSTERS

Answers: **924:** Glass! **925:** Edam. **926:** Add a 'g' to make it 'gone'. **927:** If you said toast you'd be wrong – it's bread! **928:** Longer. **929:** Silence. **930:** The surgeon is the boy's mother. **931:** Breath. **932:** Wrong.

933 Did you know there are 90 words you can spell on a basic calculator? Type in the numbers which, when you turn the screen upside down, look like letters. An easy one to start with is 0.7734, which makes 'hello'. What other words can you make?

934 What starts with a P, ends with an E, but has hundreds of letters in it?

935 A rooster lays an egg on the edge of a wall and it falls off. On which end does the egg land?

936 Ever tried creative puzzling? Stare around the room you are sitting in, then imagine that there is a deep, dark secret hidden behind a particular object that you fix your mind on. Convince your little brother that the secret is real and freak him out!

silly secret

BRILL BRAINBUSTERS

Answers: **934:** A post office. **935:** Neither, roosters don't lay eggs!

196

DAFT DARES

So, you've reached the last chapter of this book – can things get any **wackier**? Of course they can! These pages are littered with **dumb challenges** and **silly tests**. You've proved that you're a nut for silly behaviour, now it's time to rope your nearest and dearest into your **crazy schemes**, too. Do you dare to dare them?

937 Dare your friend to chew ten bits of gum at the same time.

938 Dare someone to put their toast and cereal into the blender and then drink the whizzed-up contents.

939 Dare the toughest lad you know to wear a girlie hairband into school!

940 Dare your next-door neighbour to stick a sign saying **'THEY'RE ALL MAD IN THERE'**

→

in their front window, making sure that the arrow's pointing at your place.

941 Dare your pals to run down a hill as fast as they can.

942 Dare someone to dance the macarena in the middle of your favourite shopping mall.
Heyyyyyyy macarena, yeh!

943 Dare your little brother to brush your teeth for you for an entire week. If you can stand him being that close...

TOP PRANK

945 Dare someone to approach a person in the street and say 'Excuse me, sir (even if they're a girl), what year is it?' When the person tells them, they must reply, 'Oh, no! I've miscalculated by 2 million years!' and then just run off.

944 Dare your pal to ride their bike around the park with no hands. Make sure they wear a helmet!

946 Dare a school friend to write a secret love letter to one of the teachers.

947 Dare yourself to phone a friend, adopt a silly accent and see how long it takes for them to guess it's you!

948 Dare your best friend to put on their mum's exercise gear, go into the street and start doing a crazy aerobics routine.

949 Dare a friend to slurp a full sachet of tomato ketchup.

950 Dare your show-off mate to suddenly sing 'I'm a little teapot, short and stout' in the middle of the playground. In order to win the challenge, the song must be performed with all the right actions.

951 Dare your friend to walk in your shoes for the day.

DAFT DARES

199

952 Wacky waiting room
Next time you're in the doctor's surgery, dare your brother or sis to pretend that the chair they're sitting on is a horse! Whilst sitting on the chair, get them to bluff a trot, canter and a gallop before finally getting thrown off.

SILLY SCORE

953 Dare two friends to lick each other's foot. Give marks for taste! Yuk!

954 Dare your mate to put pepper on their tongue and swallow!

956 Slob on the sofa with your best mate, then dare yourselves to probe each other's bellybuttons for fluff.

955 Dare your little bro to eat a tiny spoonful of cat food.

957 Dare your friend to eat their packed lunch without using their hands at all.

ONE-MINUTE MADNESS

Anyone reading this really should know better, but some shorties are too ridiculous to resist!

958 Dare your granny to join an Internet dating site.

959 Dare a stranger to smile at you.

960 Dare a friend to call into a radio station and sing a love song really badly on air.

961 Dare your sis to wear odd shoes for the day.

962 Dare your dad to scratch his armpit with his big toe.

964 Dare your brother to smear peanut butter all over his face and see if he can stay that way till it hardens. Warning: Don't do this if they've got a nut allergy!

963 Dare a friend to sell a pair of their used socks on an Internet auction site.

965 Dare a friend to take off their shoe and put their sock-covered foot into a clean toilet. Can they keep it there while it is flushed!?!

DAFT DARES

966 **Dare your little sister to cover her hands in your mum's fake tan.**

967 **Dare the fittest boy in your class to do 50 push-ups whilst singing the national anthem.**

968 Dare your friend to go up to someone in the playground and blow a raspberry on the back of their neck.

SILLY SCORE

969 Dare a friend to turn themselves into a human sarnie! Get two slices of bread and tell them to put them down the back of their underwear with one on each butt cheek. Can they stomach sitting on dough for 10 minutes?

970 **Dare your little brother to wear a pair of his underpants on top of his head for the day.**

YOU MUST BE JOKING!

971 **Dare your sister's friends to sit like statues for five minutes while you rub your feet in their face.**

972 Dare a friend to drink a bottle of fizzy pop as fast as they can.
BURP!

973 Dare yourself to eat a whole loaf of bread in one go. **Bleurgh!**

974 Dare someone to moonwalk backwards through your local leisure centre.

975 Dare your brother to tell your parents he doesn't believe in Christmas and absolutely doesn't want any presents this year.

976 Dare your big, mirror-lovin' teen sister to leave the house without brushing her hair.

DAFT DARES

GOLDEN OLDIES

977 How funny are your folks? Test out your parent's wacky credentials by setting them a few daft dares! Start out by challenging your dad to go next door and ask if he can borrow an ice-cube.

978 Dare your dad to swap his golf clubs with cleaning implements before going out to play golf with his pals. Has he got what it takes to putt with a mop or get a hole-in-one with a broomstick?

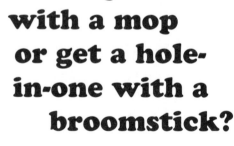

979 **Dare your mum to pick you up from school on roller skates.**

980 Dare your mum to re-enact her proposal from your dad with the roles reversed.

981 Dare your oldies to do your homework while you cook dinner. When you all sit down to eat, test your dad on fractions and ask your mum to recite your spellings off by heart.

982 **Dare your parents to learn a routine from High School Musical and perform it to their guests during their next dinner party. Wouldn't they just make the perfect Sharpay and Ryan?!!**

983 Dare your mum to pop a red sock in the wash with your dad's white work shirts. Remind her that he does look lovely in pink!!

984 Happy nappies!
Dare your parents to dress up like babies and let you parent **them** for a change. If your dad complains stuff a dummy in his mouth and send him upstairs for a nap!

985 On holiday?
Dare your parents to head to the nearest naturist beach for a spot of skinny-dipping.

986 **Dare your mum to serve you a dinner you actually like... with no vegetables at all.**

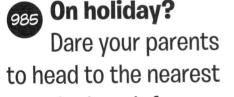

DAFT DARES

987 **Dare yourself to hang upside down from a tree branch or climbing frame for at least 30 seconds.**

988 Dare your friend to swap outfits with you and perform jumping jacks for the neighbours.

989 Next time you're going swimming, dare a boy to wear a bikini.

990 **Dare a friend to walk to school wearing a sign reading** **'I'm a dork!'**

991 Dare someone in your class to do the hand jive during a lesson or throughout an entire assembly.

992 Dare yourself to fix the prettiest girl or hunkiest boy in your school with a cross-eyed, buck-toothed stare.

DOUBLE DARE

993 Dare your sister to give your long toenails a pedicure... using her teeth as clippers.

994 Dare yourself to take one bite out of a raw potato or onion!

995 **Big mouth!**
Dare your friend to put an entire hotdog plus the roll in their mouth. Now ask them if they'd like mustard and onions!

996 **Dare someone in your class to tell the teacher that they dreamt about them last night!**

997 Dare a tone-deaf friend to enter a local talent show – or better still a national televised one!

DAFT DARES

998 A test for teacher's pet

Dare your friend to give an apple to your teacher, hug them and explain that they make coming to school worthwhile – in front of all your class mates.

999 Dare your friends to rub noses just like Inuits.

1000 Dare yourself to limbo underneath a barrier in a shopping centre.

1001 And finally... dare your best mate to wear their underpants on the outside of their clothes!